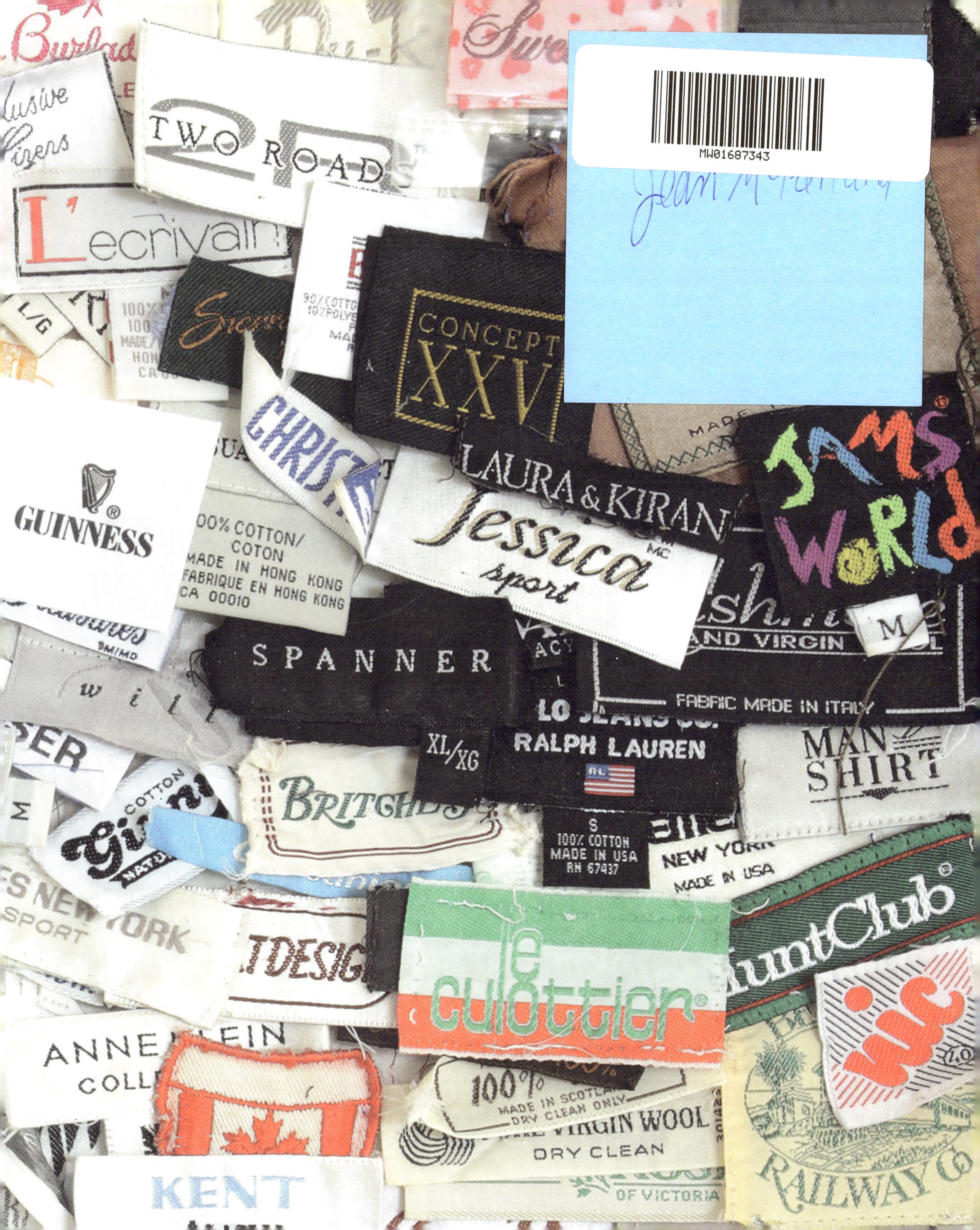
TWO ROADS
L'ecrivain
CONCEPT XXV
GUINNESS
100% COTTON/ COTON MADE IN HONG KONG FABRIQUE EN HONG KONG CA 00010
LAURA & KIRAN
Jessica sport
JAMS WORLD
SPANNER
AND VIRGIN
FABRIC MADE IN ITALY
M
XL/XG
RALPH LAUREN
S 100% COTTON MADE IN USA RN 67437
NEW YORK MADE IN USA
MAN SHIRT
BRITCHES
HuntClub
le culottier
100% MADE IN SCOTLAND DRY CLEAN ONLY
VIRGIN WOOL DRY CLEAN
OF VICTORIA
RAILWAY Co
KENT
MW01687343

CAROLE SABISTON

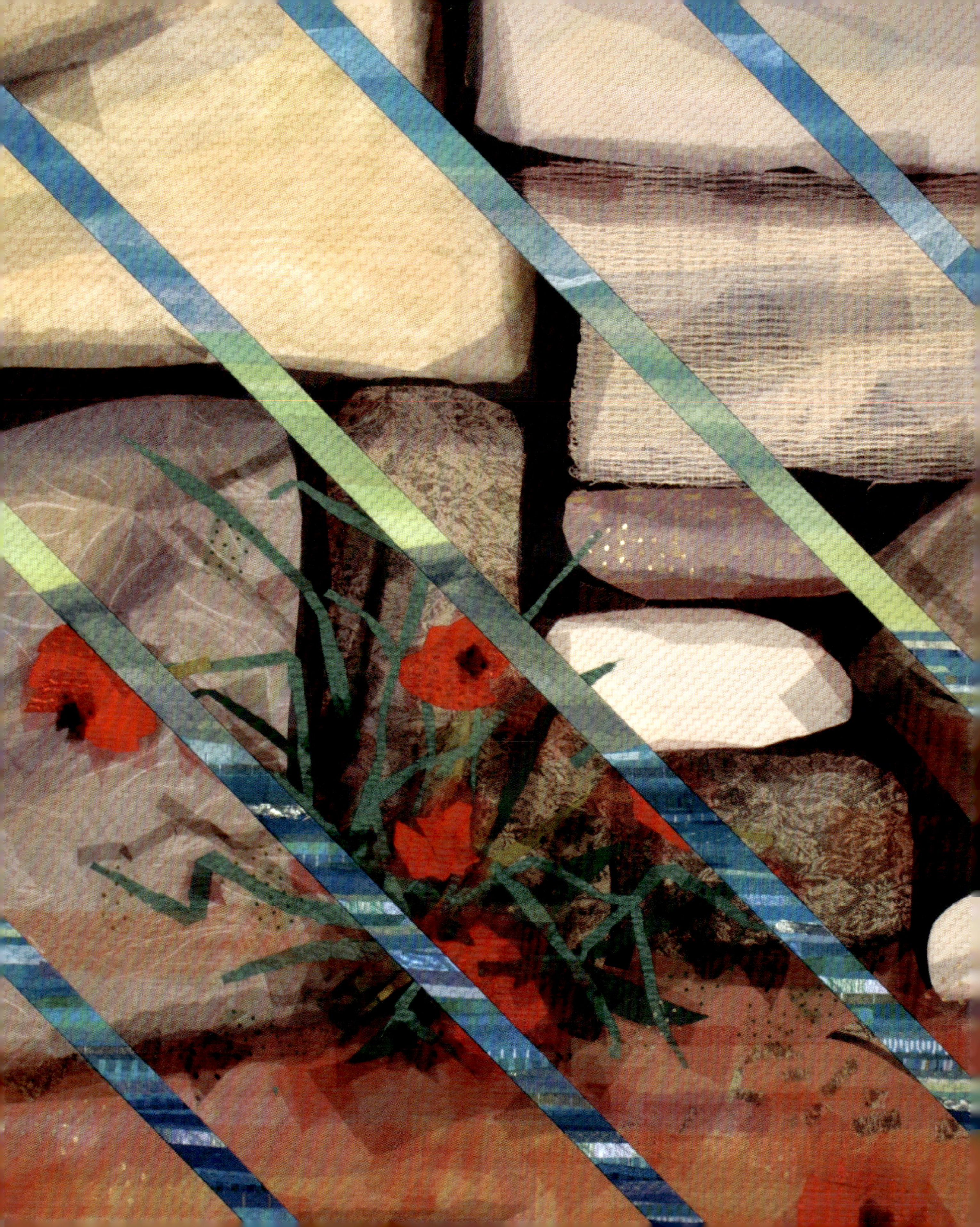

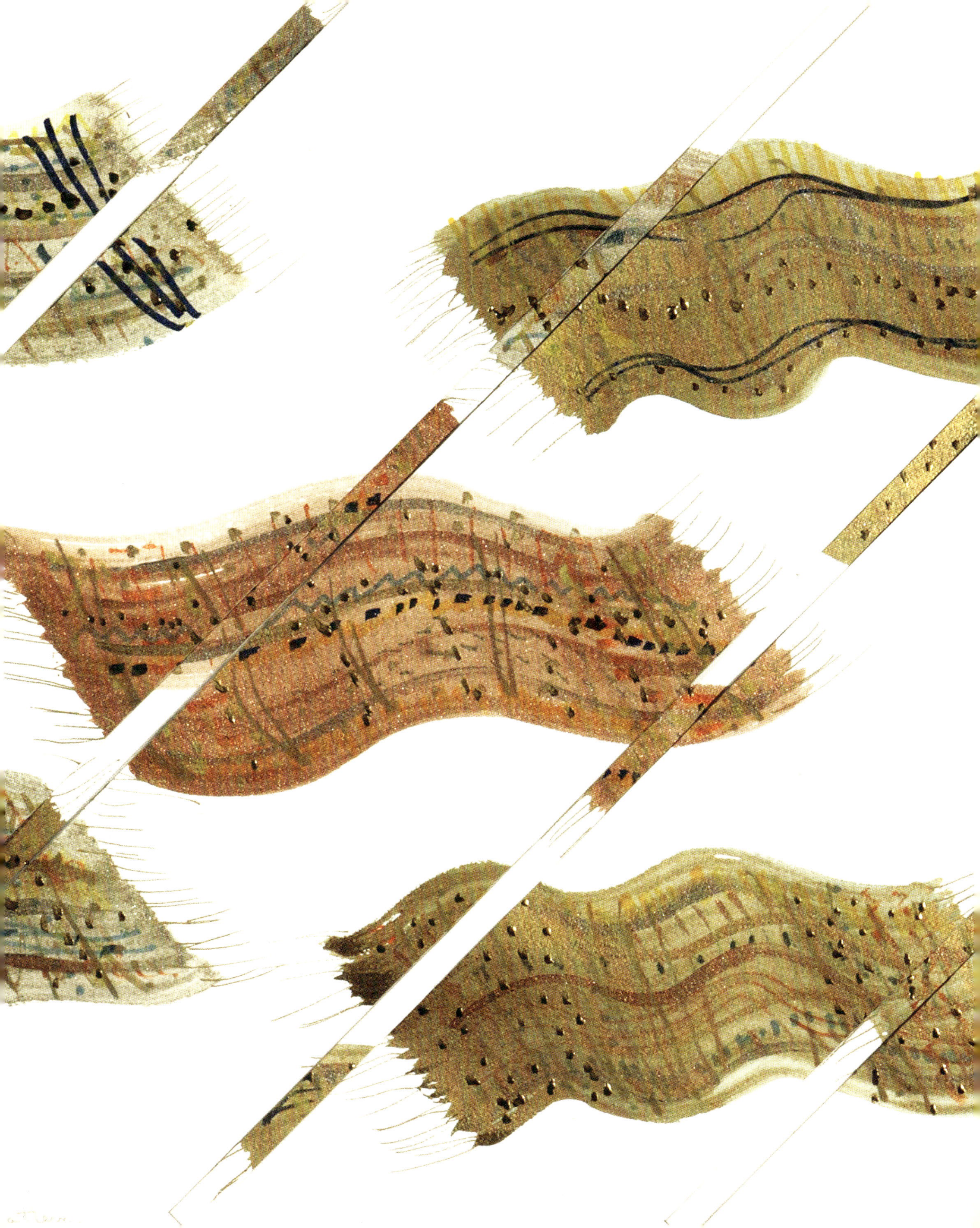

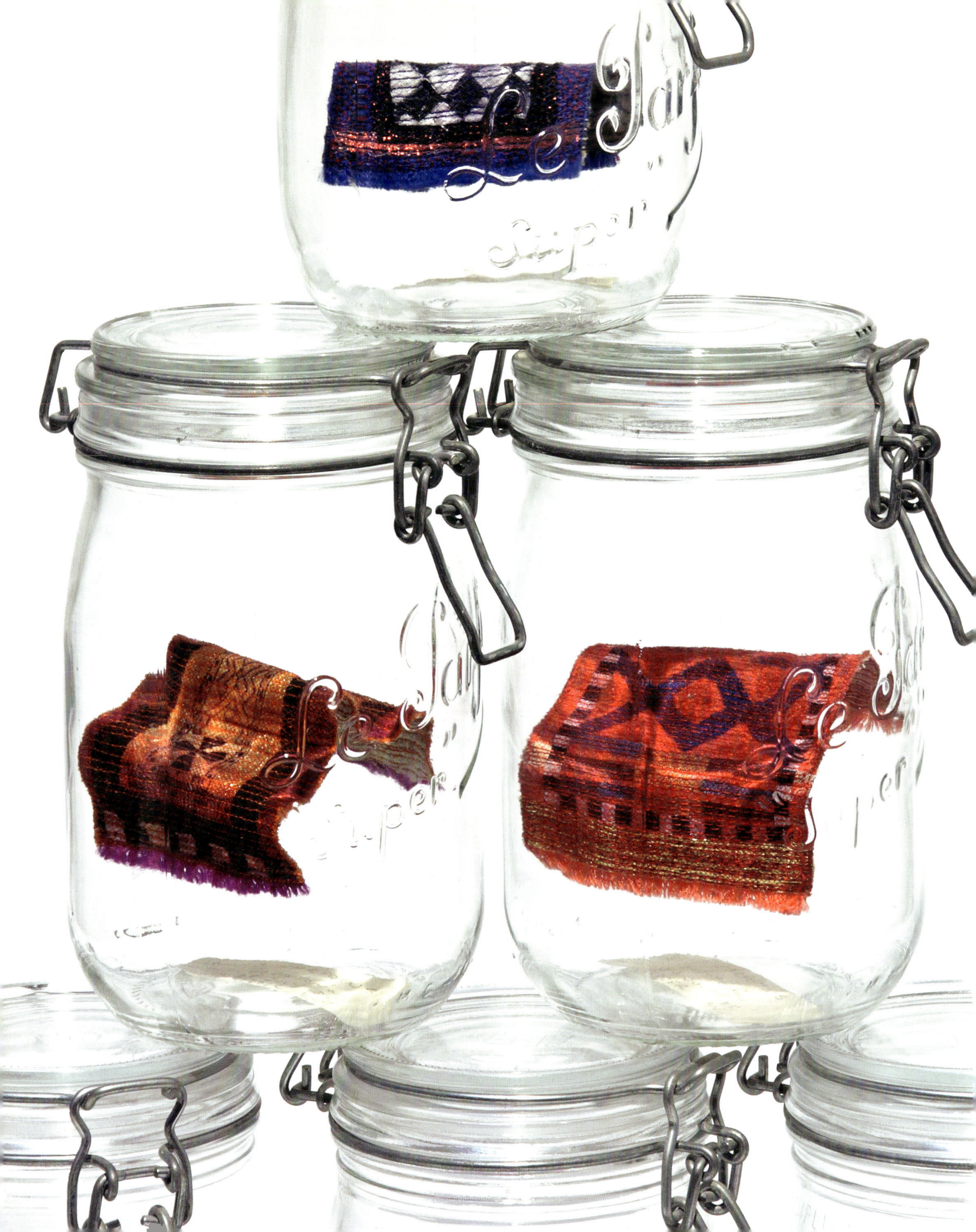

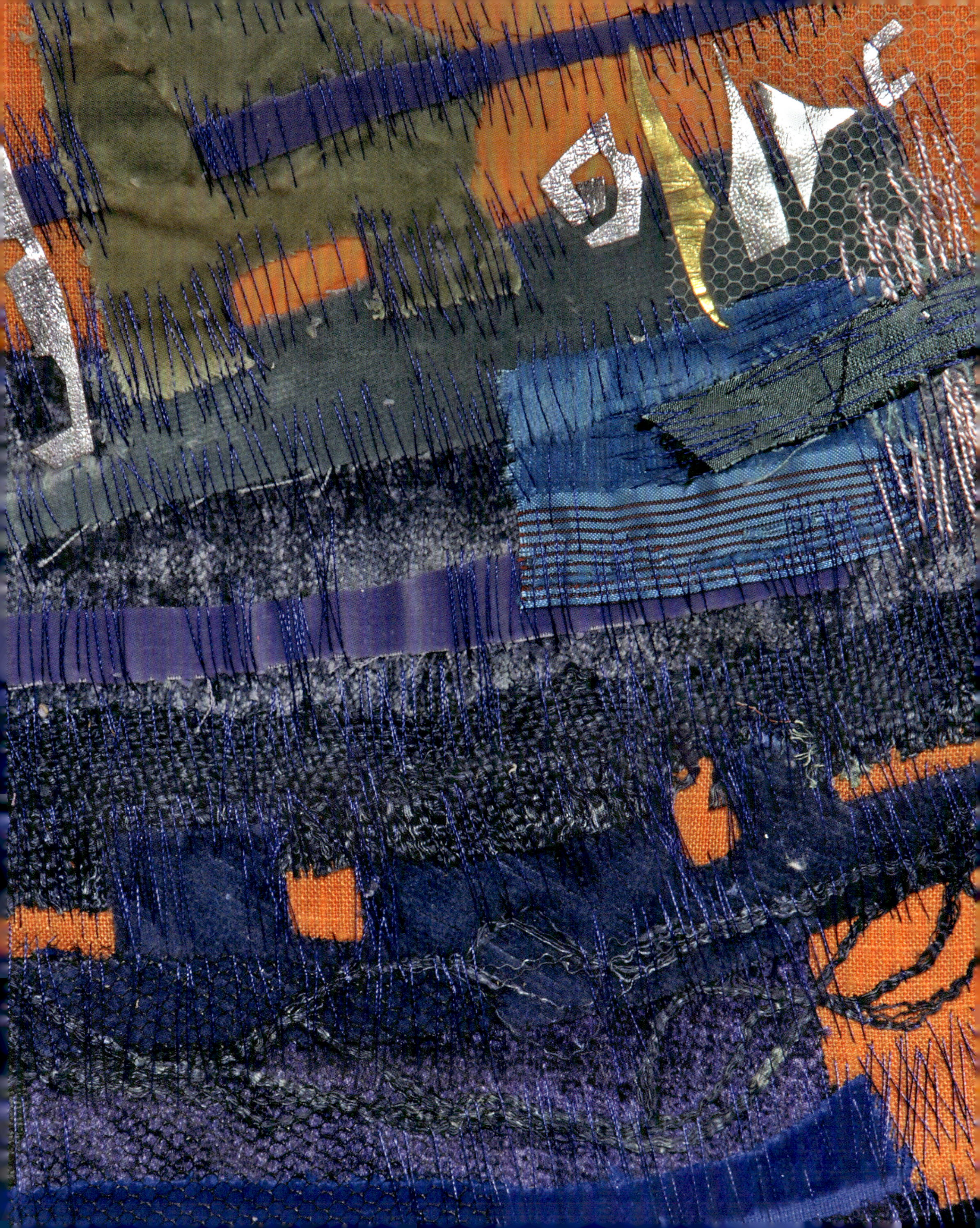

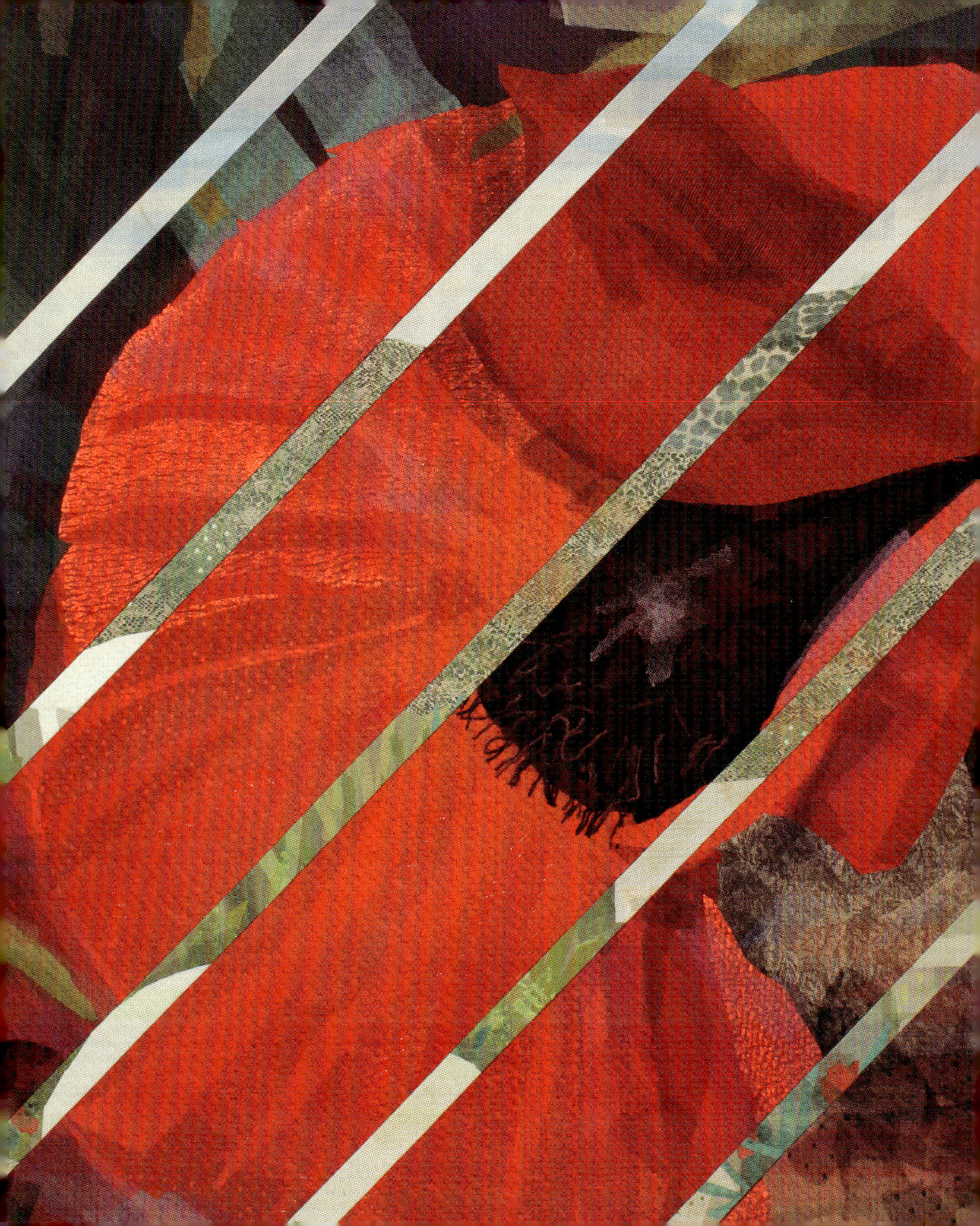

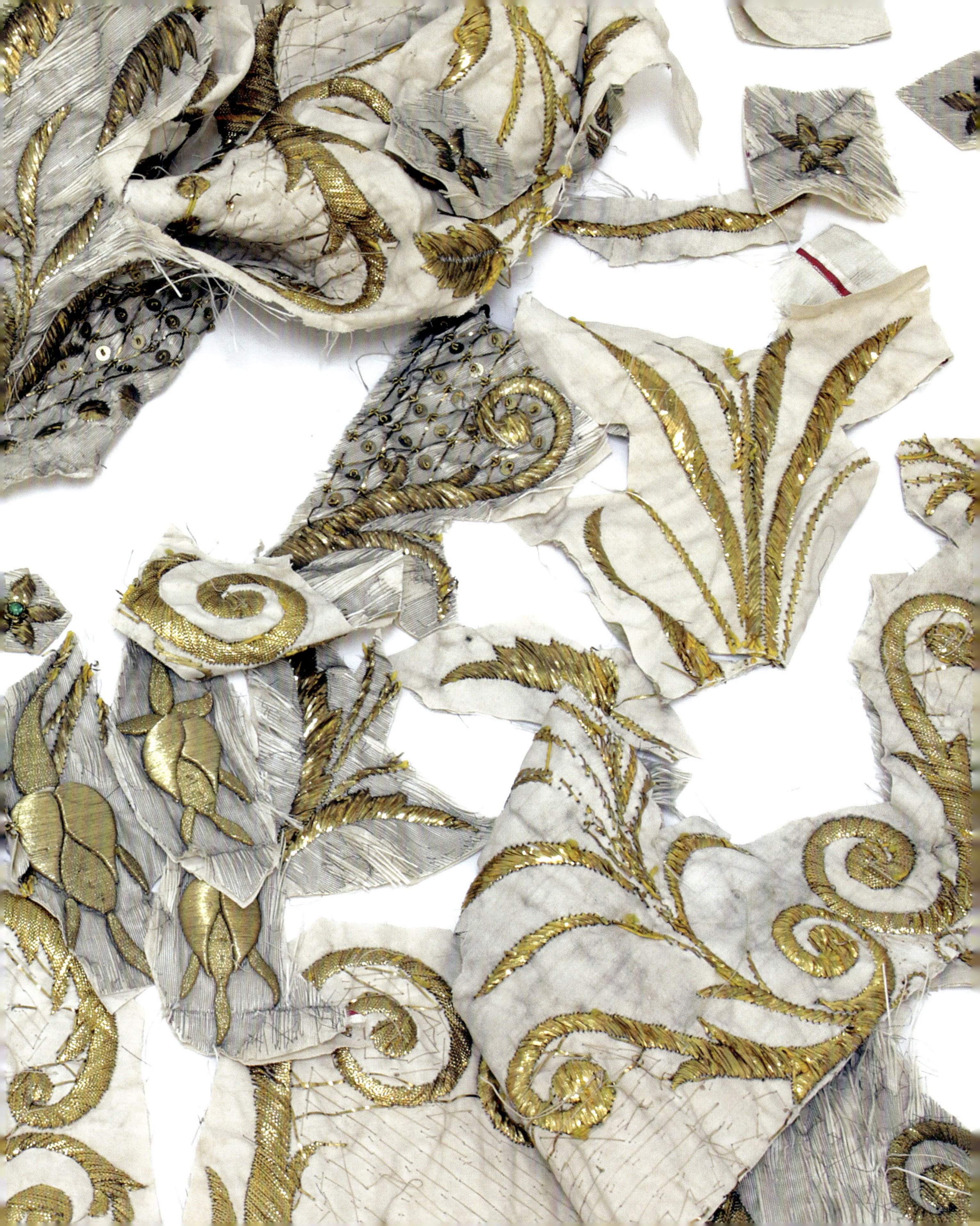

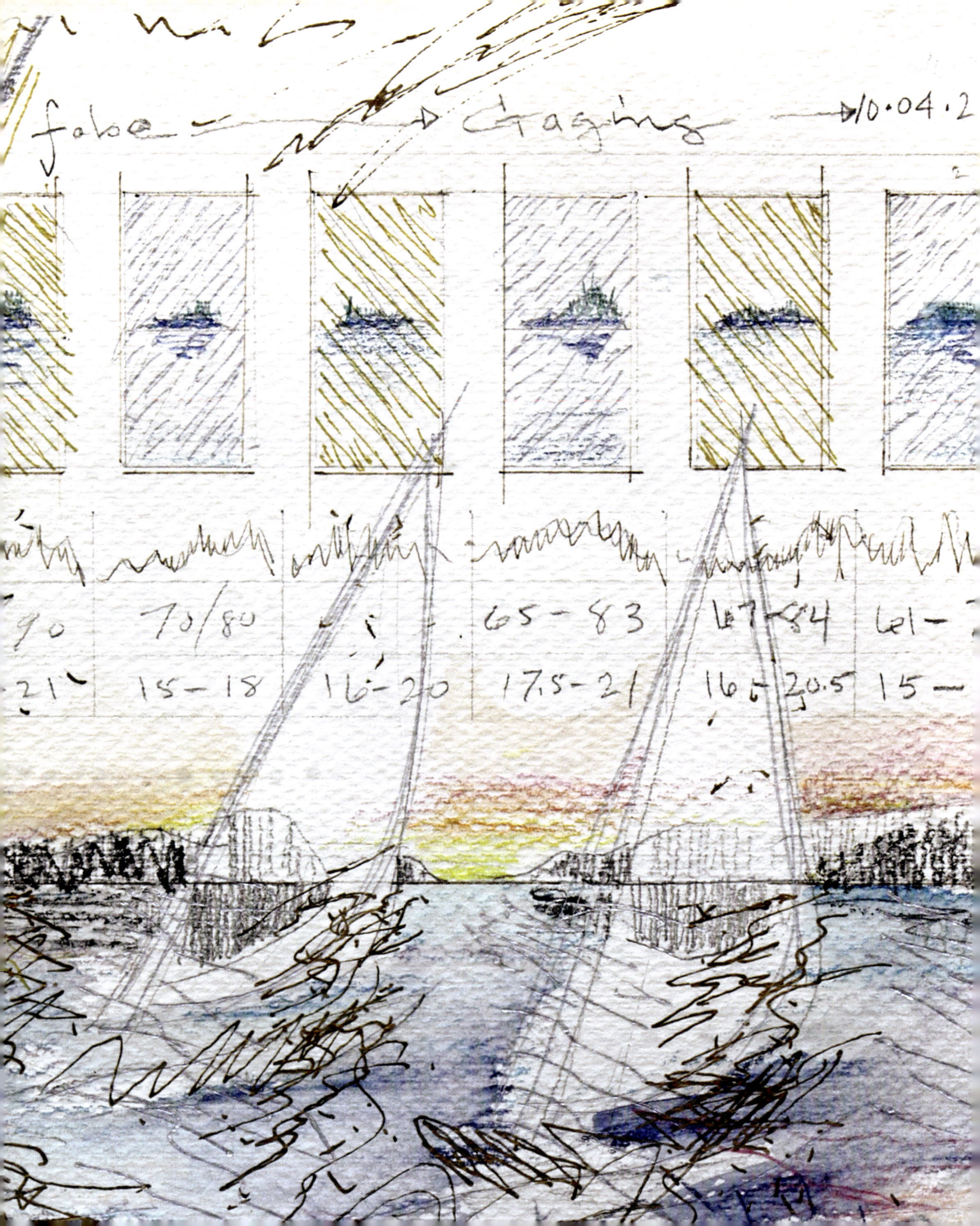
false
staging
10·04·2
70/80
65 – 83
15 – 18
16 – 20
17.5 – 21
15 –

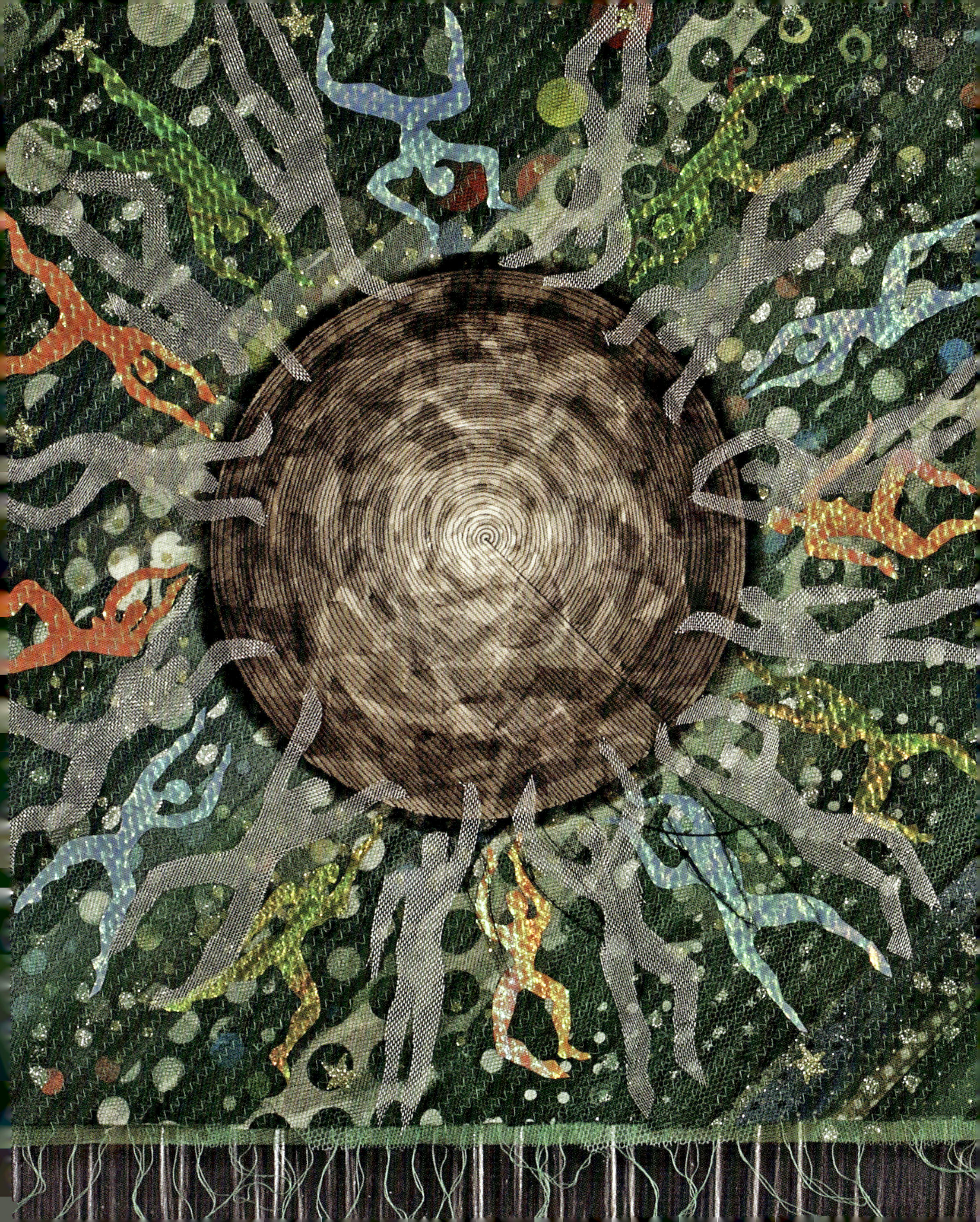

Carole Sabiston

Everything Below All of the Above

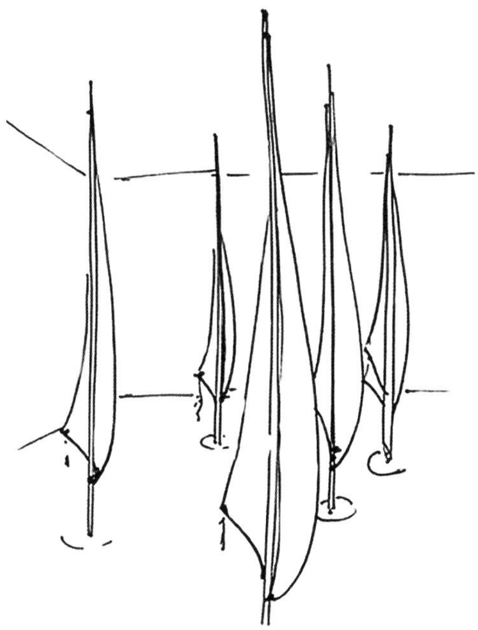

Patricia Bovey • Michelle Jacques

Art Gallery of Greater Victoria

Library and Archives Canada Cataloguing in Publication

Sabiston, Carole, 1939–
[Works. Selections]
Carole Sabiston : everything below all of the above
/ Patricia E. Bovey, Michelle Jacques.

Catalogue of an exhibition held at the Art Gallery of Greater Victoria, January 24 to April 28, 2014.

ISBN 978-0-88885-374-5 (bound)

1. Sabiston, Carole, 1939– —Exhibitions. I. Bovey, Patricia E., writer of added text II. Jacques, Michelle, writer of added text III. Art Gallery of Greater Victoria, issuing body, host institute IV. Title.

N6549.S22A4 2014   709.2   C2013-907618-2

Printed in Canada

FRONT COVER

cat. 25 *Everything Below: All of the Above*, 2003

BACK COVER

The Artist in Her Studio, 1985
Background work:
The Water Music Suite, 1985

ENDSHEETS

Collected Labels:
Elements for future works

DETAILS PAGES 2–9

cat. 21 *Flying into Delos* (detail), 1992

cat. 40 *Flying Carpets Study #5* (detail), 1990

cat. 22 *Magicus Carpetus: Squadron – Preserving a Flying Tradition* (detail), 1992

cat. 2 *Colour Study: Blue Rain* (detail), 1976

cat. 21 *Flying into Delos* (detail), 1992

Fragments, 18th-century Spanish cope, used in *Flying Rufus*, 2009

cat. 44 *Weather Systems* (detail), 2000

cat. 24 *Flying Revolution Quartet* (lower right quadrant), 1993

TITLE PAGE

cat. 35 *Study for Sailing #1* (detail), 1982

OPPOSITE PAGE

Carole Sabiston, 1985

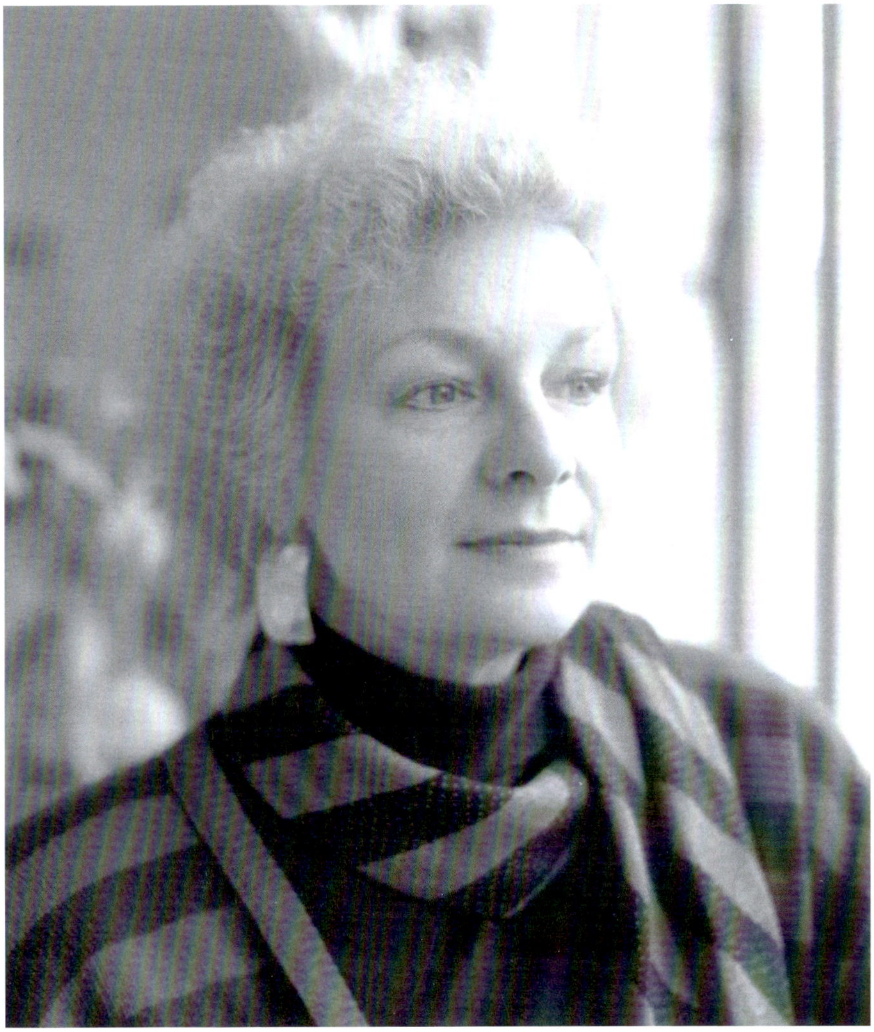

contents

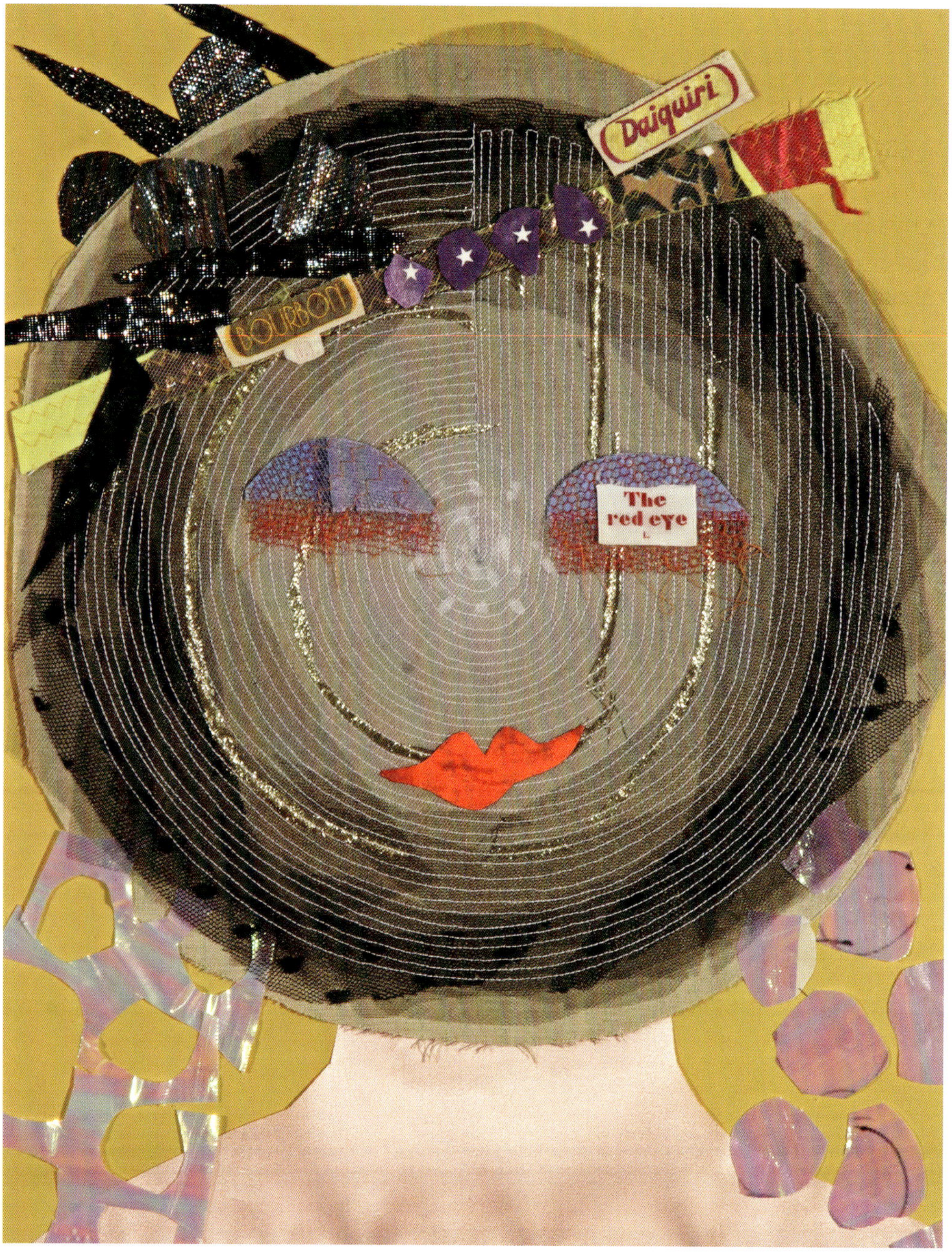
Daiquiri
BOURBON
The
red eye

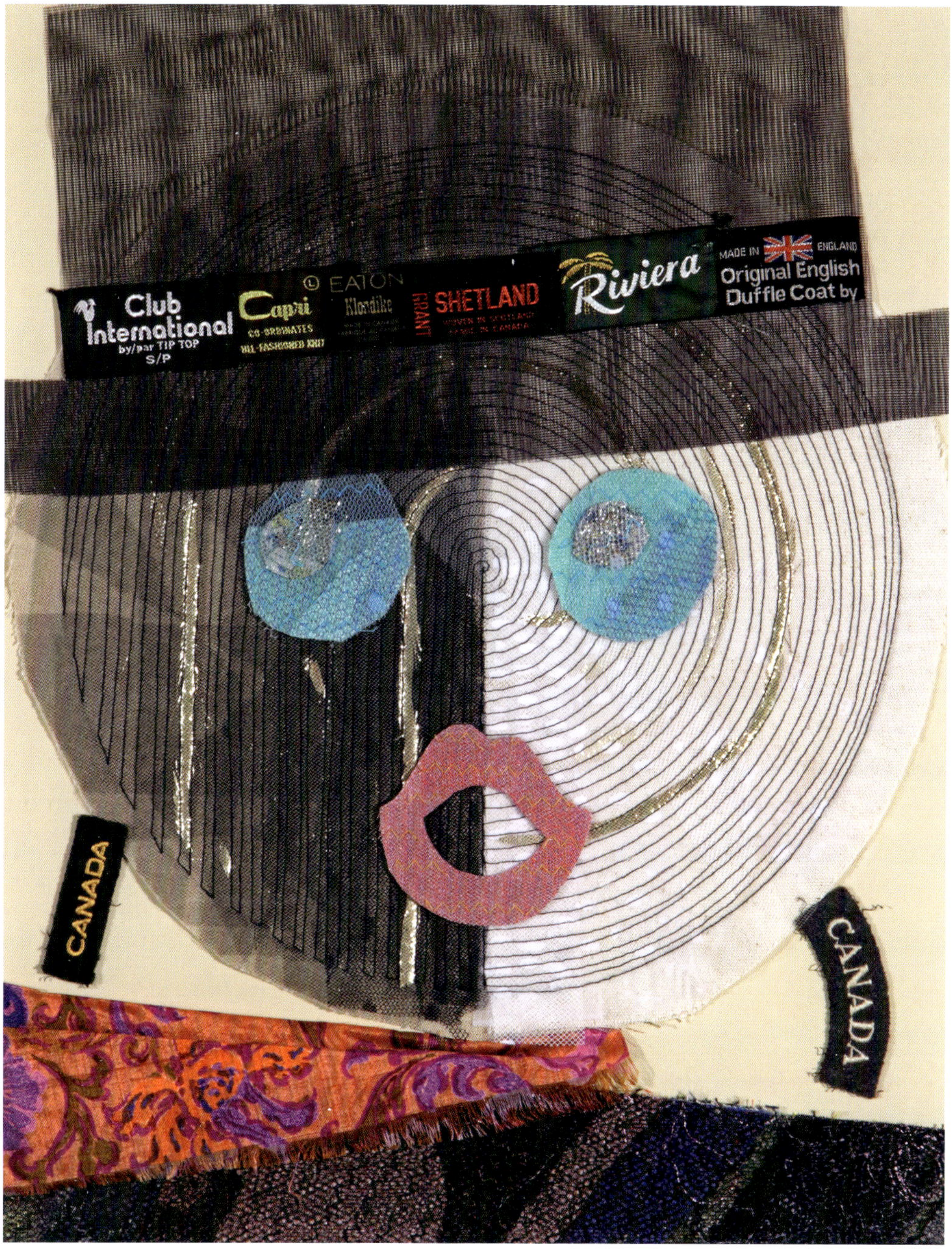
Club International
by/par TIP TOP
S/P
Capri
EATON
Klondike
GRANT
SHETLAND
Riviera
MADE IN ENGLAND
Original English
Duffle Coat by
CANADA
CANADA

PREVIOUS SPREAD

cat. 11 *Self Portrait: The Cocktailer*, 1984

cat. 14 *Self Portrait: The Traveller*, 1984

OPPOSITE PAGE

Carole Sabiston working on *Sailing*, 1981

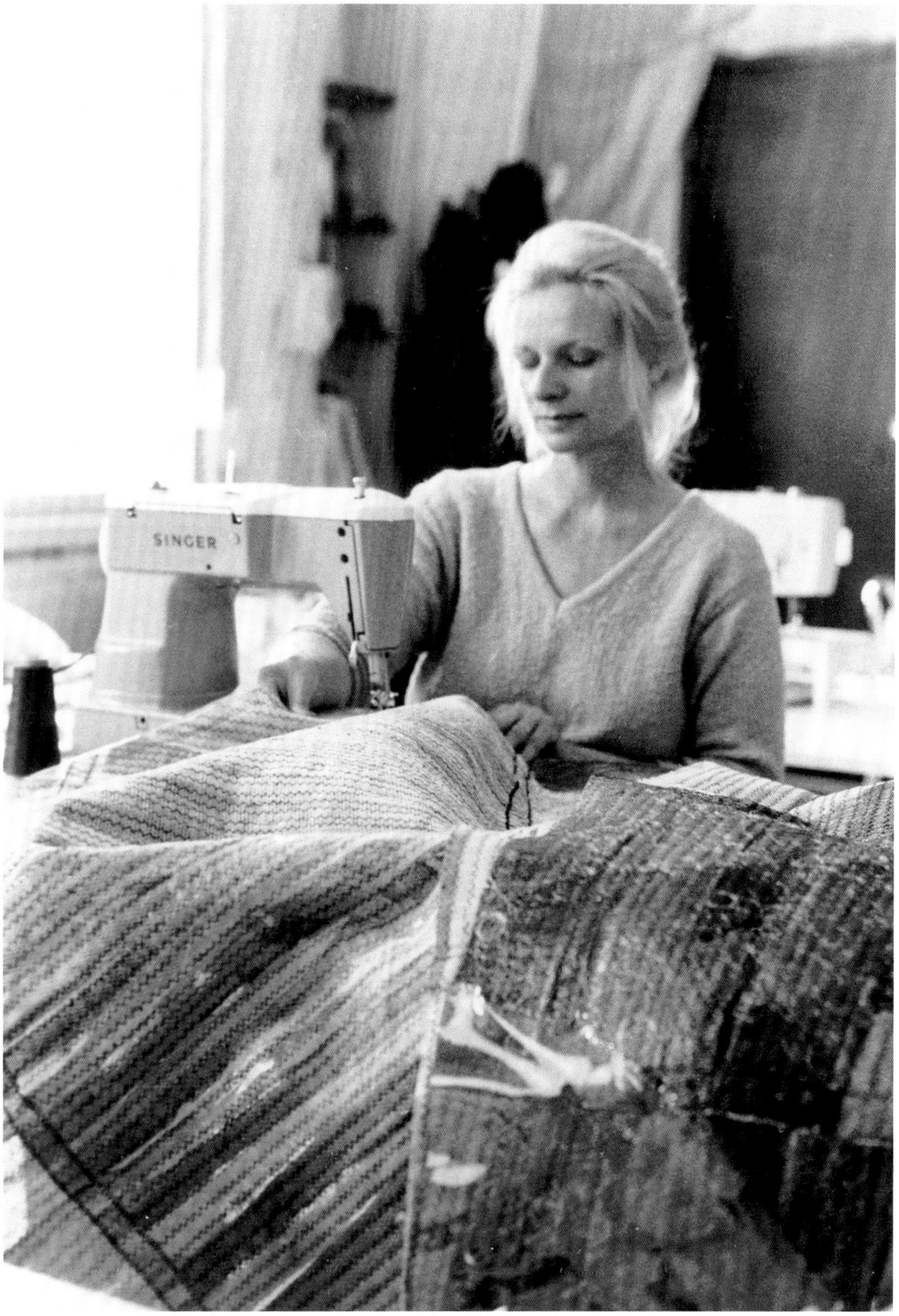
SINGER

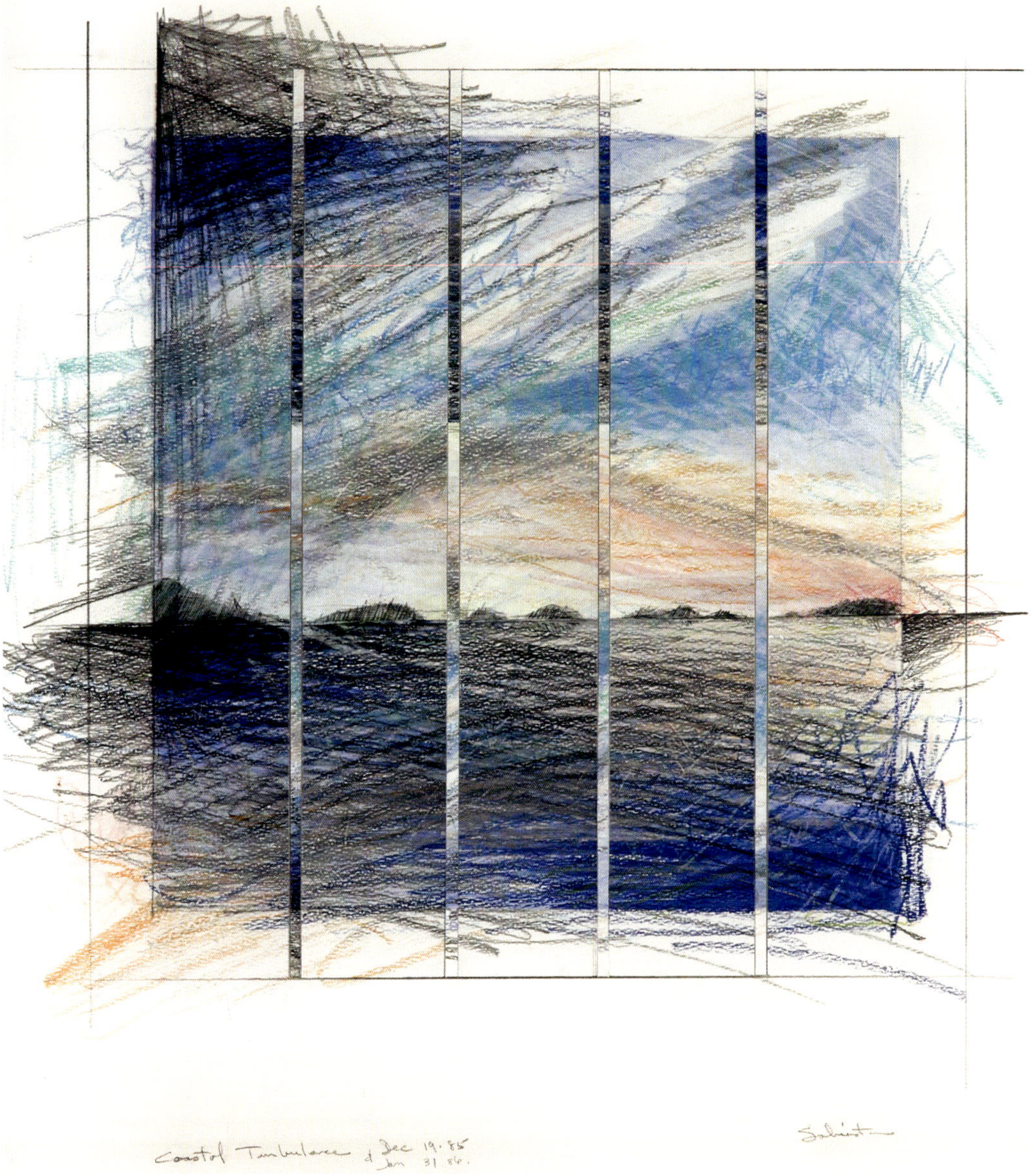

cat. 41 *Coastal Turbulence #1*, 1985/86

Director's Foreword

Carole Sabiston: Everything Below All of the Above celebrates Sabiston's artistic production over the course of her more than forty-year career. With works intimate and monumental, drawn from private and public holdings and the artist's own collection, the selection, skillfully curated by Patricia Bovey, conveys the remarkable range of invention of a creative hand that challenged the expectations of the textile medium while capitalizing on its familiarity and universal appeal. Together, the exhibition and this publication, which features a major text by Bovey and a contextualization of the artist's inspirations from, and impact on, art history by AGGV chief curator Michelle Jacques, provide the most comprehensive analysis of Sabiston's work to date.

This project bears, undeniably, the mark of a curator in possession of a long and meaningful connection with the artist. An art historian, writer, educator and consultant now based in Winnipeg, Bovey was the director of the AGGV from 1980 through 1999. Bovey's relationship with Sabiston spans most of the artist's career, and it was with great enthusiasm that we engaged in the development of this project with her, knowing that it would result in a beautiful and insightful consideration of the artist's production. I extend thanks and admiration to my respected colleague and predecessor.

Carole Sabiston: Everything Below All of the Above would not have been possible without the participation of lenders both public and private, and it is with sincere gratitude that I acknowledge their generosity. Also essential to the realization of this project were the efforts of the AGGV staff, as well as John Taylor, who so sensitively photographed most of the work reproduced here, and Frank Reimer, who designed this stunning publication.

We are also deeply grateful for the ongoing support of the Capital Regional District, the BC Arts Council and the Canada Council for the Arts, and to the Associates of the Art Gallery of Greater Victoria, who provided additional financial support for this project.

Above all, though, I would like to extend my gratitude to Carole Sabiston, of course for creating her remarkable body of work, but also for being a true leader of the arts in our community. We offer this exhibition and publication as an invitation to all of our visitors to celebrate the renowned accomplishments of our dear friend, and to encounter new revelations in her work.

Jon Tupper
Director, AGGV

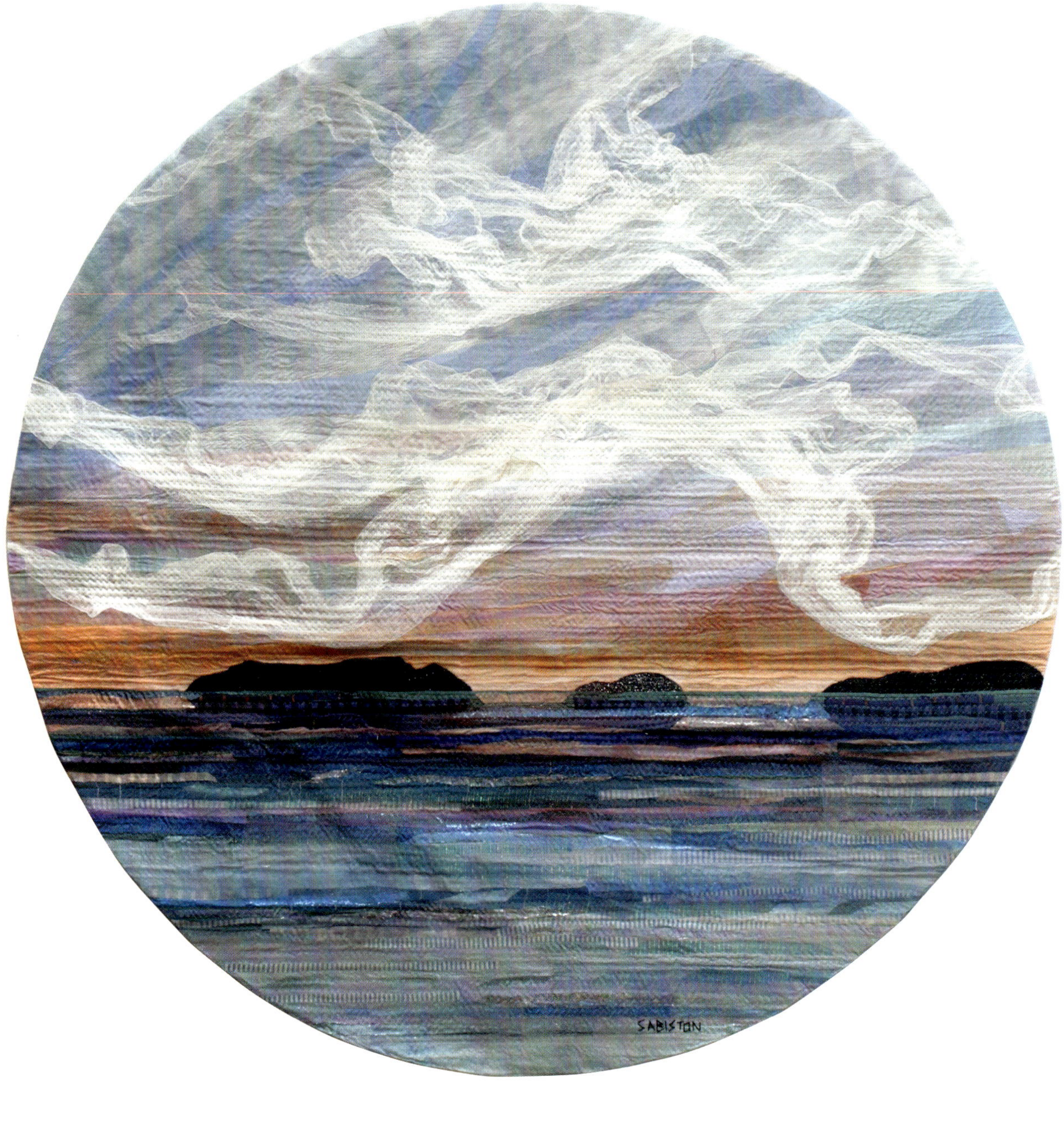
SABISTON

PATRICIA BOVEY

Carole Sabiston: Everything Below All of the Above

I hope each person can find some sort of freedom in my art.

—Carole Sabiston, in *Art on Video: The Art of Carole Sabiston* (1990)

Fanciful Yet Resolute Foretelling

Carole Sabiston, textile assemblage artist of national and international acclaim, has developed a unique visual language over many years. Rich colours, textures and movement fuse to create immediately engaging works filled with fantasy and humour. Her work of the past fifty years has conveyed serious environmental issues affecting our global future while pointing to lost ways of life. She draws from histories that should not be forgotten, and also from world literature and contemporary commentaries.

Everything Below: All of the Above (2003), the cover image for this publication, ties many elements in the artist's oeuvre together—light, movement, space, colour, flying, myriad objects, labels and text. Her visual integrity eloquently unites natural and imaginary references as one. Visually, technically and philosophically, Sabiston reveals tensions and dichotomies in the world around us. She ably juxtaposes the neat and tidy bits of life and the universe with the unfinished, and continuous motion with ongoing unresolved questions, deftly superimposing the natural and the unnatural.

cat. 17 *The Flying Rondels at Dawn*, 1987

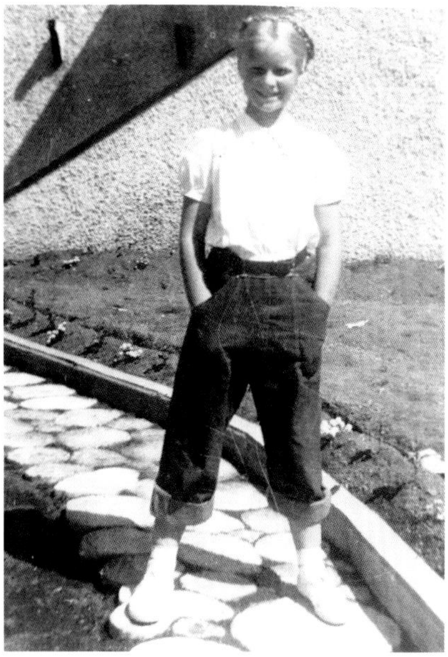

Emigrating from a small community in England at the age of eight, she and her parents arrived at Pier 21 in Halifax in January 1948 and immediately embarked on the iconic train trip across Canada, finally settling in British Columbia. The trip, both at sea and over land, made an indelible impact on the young Carole. The sense of the horizon line across the ocean and prairies, and the constantly changing light as they travelled west, have had career-long subconscious effects on her work, as have the coastal lights, skies and water. The horizon anchors her inventive compositions, in which silent travel, movement and flight continuously interweave reality and dreams.

Images with multiple meanings juxtapose the serious and the fanciful. Her technique, too, is filled with contrasts. It is free yet detailed, deliberate and meticulous, every work combining the macro and the micro. She invites and challenges her viewers to come with her on her imaginary journeys.

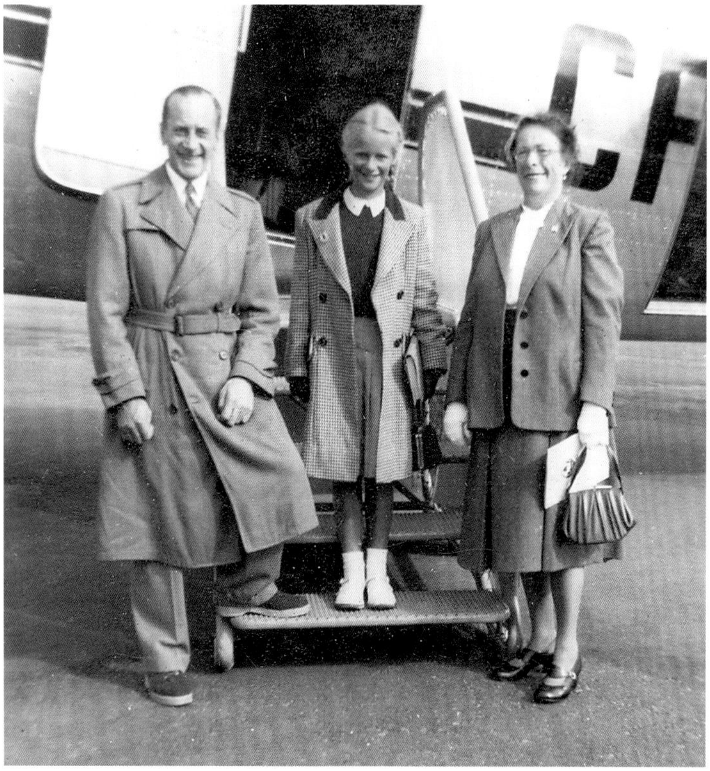

The "Jean Girl," age 11, in West Vancouver, 1951

First flight—the artist at 11 with her father, George Slater, and her grandmother, Nanny Clegg, 1951

Underpinnings & Overviews

Bringing image and process together provides the challenge I relish.

—Carole Sabiston in conversation with Patricia Bovey (May 23, 2013)

Using multiple layers of textiles, thick and thin, rough and smooth, matte and metallic, the artist builds her pieces. Translucent and opaque passages are superimposed in each work to create shifting lights, evoking the continuous shimmering effects in water and air.

Through her career, Sabiston has worked in various studios—large rented lofts in old-town Victoria; an upper floor in Munro's Books on Government Street; and latterly in the architect-designed studio at her home. A skylight with remote screening gives her a view of the sky, the treetops and passing clouds while letting her control the desired level of light. All her studios have been methodically organized, lively, creative spaces replete with the accoutrements required for the work in production. In the middle of her home studio is a large modular work table that is flexible in shape and size. She places her cutting systems and layout screens on it as needed. An industrial sewing machine is in a corner, and racks of large and small plastic containers filled with colour-sequenced materials are stacked against the wall and under the table. She keeps particularly interesting remnants and vintage pieces for the "right" project. Fragments from an eighteenth-century Spanish gold cope with richly embroidered flowers and stars, for instance, became integral elements in her 2002 commission of the *Reredos* for Victoria's Christ Church Cathedral, and other bits of the same cope became symbolic details in *Flying Rufus* (2009) and *Planet Earth: After P. K. Page* (2013). Likewise, boxes of antique French silk threads, squirrelled away for a number of decades, were recently incorporated as a key component in *Connecting Threads: Arc of Carol Shields* (2013), her personal remembrance of Carol Shields.

Running along one studio wall is a bookshelf filled with reference resources, her archives and various volumes about the work of friends. The lower shelves contain portfolios of drawings, photographs, ideas for commissions, and more. In the corner is her computer, the artist's link to the wider world.

Sabiston has never been short of visual possibilities. A single studio visit quickly proves her imaginative and constant flow of thoughts. Works in progress, photographs, scraps of material, magazine and newspaper clippings that captured her imagination, and her quick coloured pencil sketches are pinned onto her cork walls. Some of these bear rudimentary colour notes. Pinned or stapled to others are sample strips of materials she is considering for inclusion in the final work. Her sketches often have descriptions of her intent—size, scope, interesting quotes or poignant phrases from letters she has received over the years. Larger working sketches are replete with glass-headed colour pins attaching photos, various textile pieces, colours and other sundry elements.

Why pinning, which she refers to as "pinning to stay"?[1] Do the pins, in her mind, mean the composition is set or fixed? Is pinning the final stage in defining her idea? Or do the pins suggest fluidity? Will the composition change, move or shift completely? How does this pinning relate to her next step of cutting and slicing her images and turning parts upside down and regrouping them? The splicing and reversing of strips imbue her compositions with strong parallel lines of force. These lines of force, like those in the paintings of the Italian Futurist artists of the early twentieth century, take the eye through the work and beyond the picture plane—for the eye of the viewer, silent travel continues.

Sabiston's work is painterly. She began her artistic career as a painter and returned to the medium for a couple of years in the 1990s. In both her painting forays, she enjoyed the immediacy of the medium. When she delved deeply, however, she found painting did not, and could not, allow her to achieve the effects she desired—those effects of light, transparency and uninhibited movement. Nonetheless, she liked the ease with which she could manipulate light and shade in paint. That experience as a painter gave her textile assemblages added depth and shading, chiaroscuro effects in fabric akin to those in the paintings of Italian old masters.

Sabiston began working seriously with textiles in the 1960s, and her first major solo exhibition, *Stitcheries by Carole Sabiston*, was at the Art Gallery of Greater Victoria in June 1967, a year after she returned to Victoria from London, Ontario, with her young son. From that point on she developed her own innovative approach and use of materials. This shift to her self-devised technique and her own visual symbols meant she stood alone as a pioneer in Canada. "It was unique in its time. There was nobody doing what Carole was doing."[2]

The artist is deliberate in the manner and intensity with which she conceives each work. Nothing is left to accident. She uses found objects, labels, scarves, gloves, collars, lace and myriad other bits, each carefully selected for symbolic or biographical reasons, or both. Multiple layers add multiple meanings and increased reflection. *Myriad Voices* (1973) exemplifies how, even in those first years, she was building her work in layers. She uses her diversity of materials as other artists have used collage, papiers collés or stencilled words. Early in her career she did her stitching by hand, deftly manipulating her threads much as Edgar Degas handled his pastels. The work of Degas, particularly his depictions of movement that defy gravity, resonates with Sabiston, a dancer for many years.

In 1979, however, she began to use the industrial sewing machine. The five-panelled *Japan Journey* (1979) is an important transitional work from hand to machine stitching. Done following her first trip to Japan, this work is filled with the many visual delights and sensibilities that captured her eye and imagination—bamboo, kimonos, Tori gates, Sumo wrestlers and the light, colours and shapes of Japan. Each of the panels is a scroll, recalling Japanese scroll paintings of many centuries. She says, "[I] wanted to work faster; I had so many ideas I had to work faster. *Japan Journey* set me free."[3] Since 1979 her works have grown in size, scope and complexity.

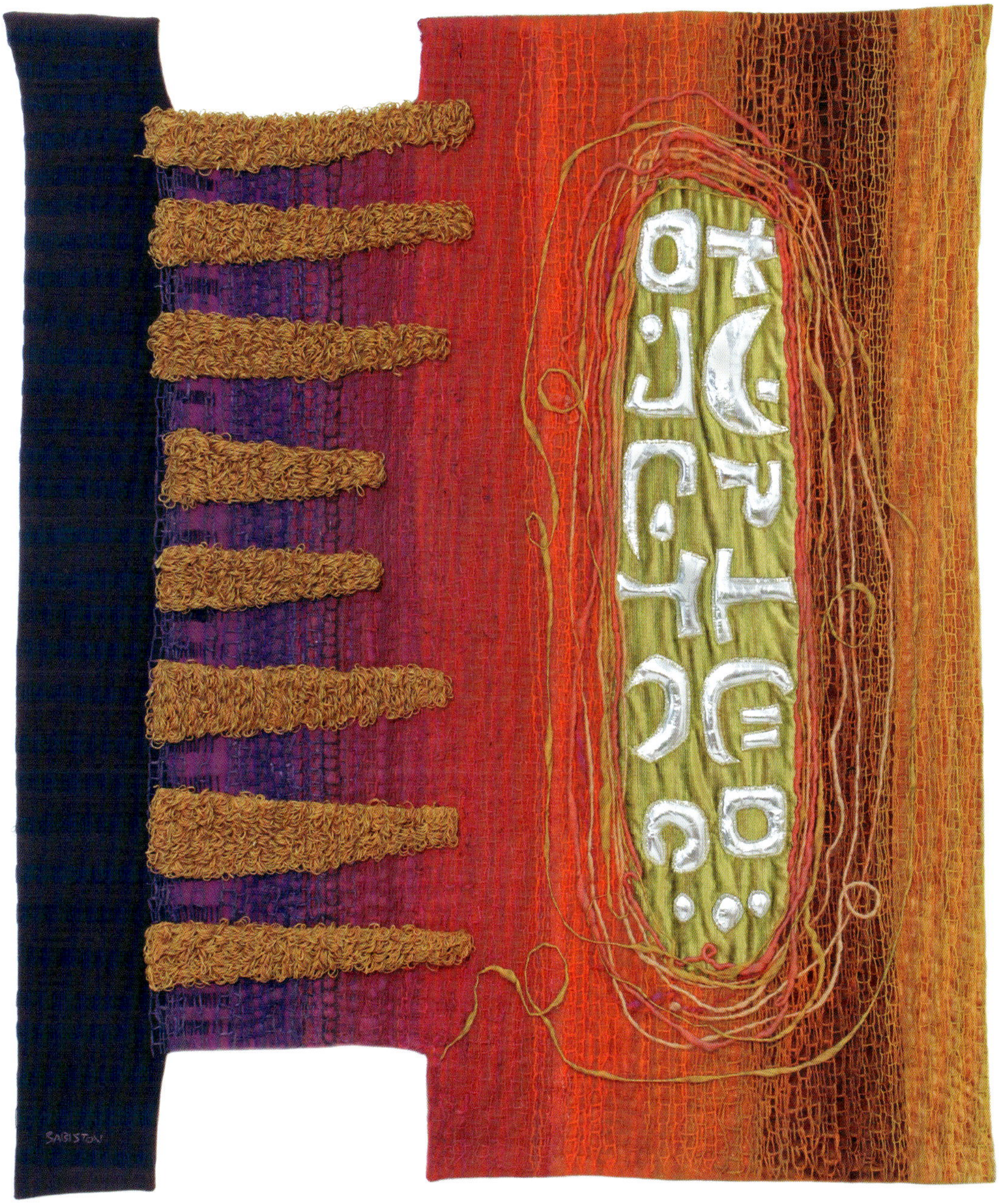

cat. 1 *Myriad Voices*, 1973

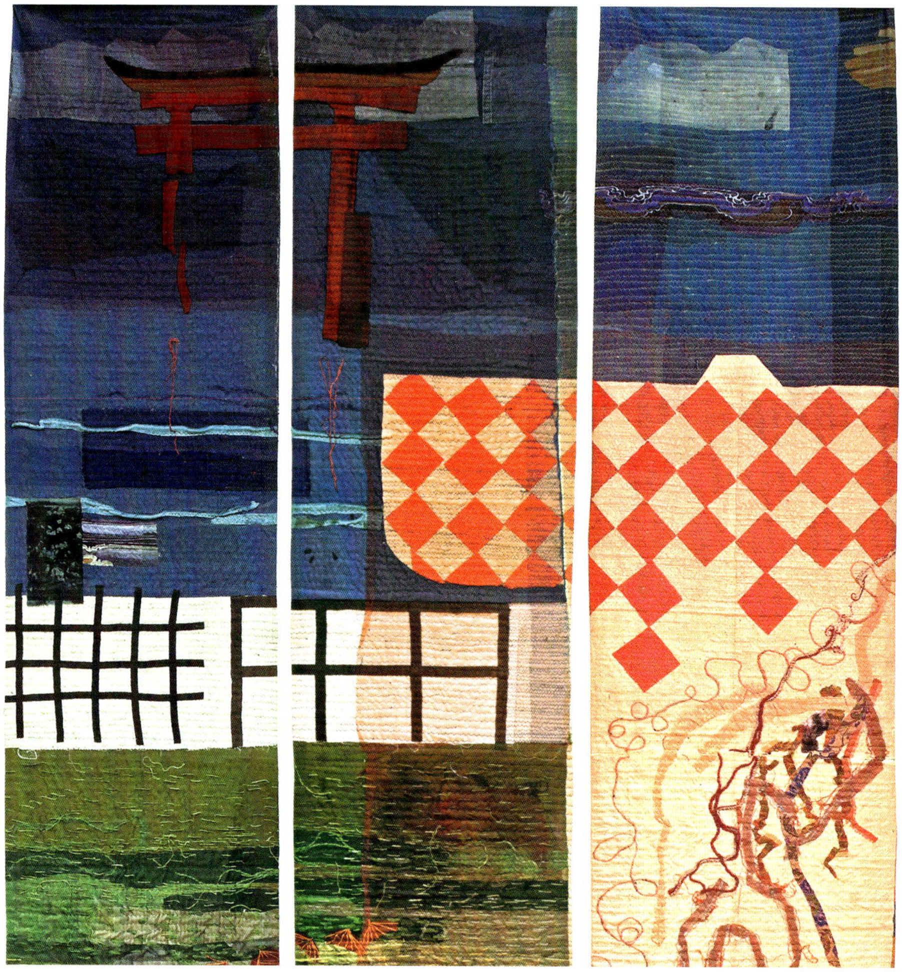

cat. 4
Japan Journey (detail), 1979

Canadian poet P.K. Page reflected on the fact that Sabiston's approach was initially derived from the traditional world of women, from seamstresses to the kitchen:

> *the stuff of a woman's life—the fabrics, the needle and thread, and...jam jars...but there is nothing literal about her use of these things. She expands it...something totally new has taken over. With this change of scale from small to almost immeasurable...something clearly has happened inside her head that is different.*[4]

That difference in her head and art was significant. From 1979 forward, Sabiston's work elegantly binds the wider universe, past, present and future, with the specificity of the minutiae of the individual. Her threads interweave the many issues, ideas, joys and sensibilities she explores. They illuminate the interconnectedness of everything, above and below, revealing the frayed edges we as human beings leave around us. Sabiston captures that dichotomous reality consistently and poignantly. In some works, like *Connecting Threads: Arc of Carol Shields*, the threads are much more than just the "technique"; they are part of the subject.

Sabiston is keen that her process and the "workings" of her art be transparent; she does not hide how she creates what she does. She wants her viewers to understand what she has done and how she has done it: "I have always left my structure visible; I don't try to hide it. I suppose it's like contemporary architecture, like the Pompidou Museum in Paris. The structure is visible; all the conduits are outside."[5]

Barbara Lee Smith, in her publication *Celebrating the Stitch: Contemporary Embroidery of North America*, describes Sabiston's technique:

> *First she draws the position of the sections on a heavy Pellon backing. Next, fabrics, from large shapes to tiny snippets, are laid out in one go... each piece of fabric is settled and smoothed into place. Once the work is laid out, all the pieces and the overlying net are pinned with glass-headed pins. Those first positioning lines are now covered by the bits of fabric, so it is necessary to remark the placement by laying string over them...Using the string as a guide, she cuts out the sections. Each section is machine sewn with a wide zigzag stitch, which holds the fabric and net to the Pellon ground. Smaller strips are now cut from these wider sections, which ultimately will form the diagonal bands seen in most of her work. These strips are about 6 inches wide at the outset, but with 4 inches allowed for seams, only 2 inches are left visible. Once cut, they are either reversed in place or worked into another panel of the same piece. Now that it is cut apart, the whole piece must be put back together. Technically, the matching and seam-making must be exact. With every 4 inches lost every time a strip or section is cut and re-sewn, Sabiston must consider how this will affect the design.*[6]

This mathematical aspect of Sabiston's work is exacting. Her measurements have to be correct or her image, its movement and message will be severely compromised. She has used that same compositional approach in some paper works, such as *Flying Carpets #1, #3, #4* and *#5* (1990), in which she sliced the diagonals and collated them back into the whole, reversing their original directions.

Once her overall idea has been formulated, the choice of materials and additional elements as background, dominant colours, details and reinforcing symbols becomes paramount for the artist:

> *The appeal of fabric for Sabiston is in its mundane quality, and she recognizes that cloth is often less accepted in the art world because of that quality..."I've always thought of the recycling process: things that were never thrown away. I suppose that comes from the original quilting idea. Every square inch was to be reused. I keep fabrics right down to the smallest pieces."*[7]

This is germane for all her works, early and late. Barbara Lee Smith comments that Sabiston's "assemblages of mundane fabric, remnants, the 'fragments of society' unite through her vision the earthly world and the vastness of space."[8] Sabiston is insistent on using everyday objects and materials

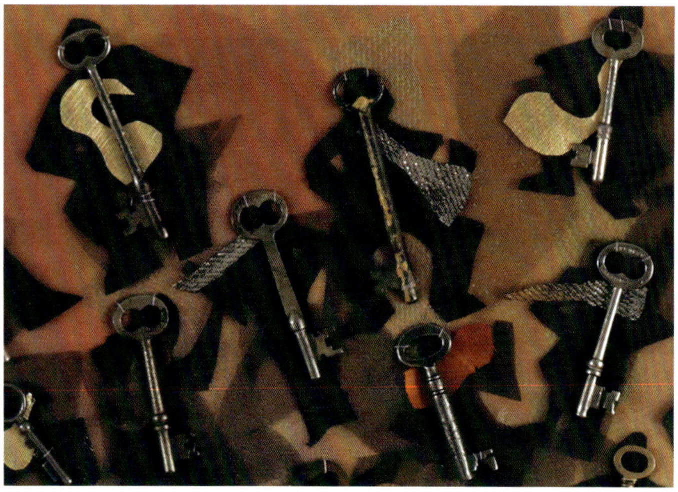

cat. 29
Opus #1:
In the Key of ?
(detail), 2009

without any mystery behind them. Men's ties, labels, trouser pockets and sundry clothing items are incorporated into her assemblages for reasons specific to the intent of the work. They link personal and intimate connections with larger universal ones. A tie, for instance, might once have belonged to an individual connected with the commission; labels are chosen for words particularly apt to the work's mood and meaning. In *Connecting Threads: Arc of Carol Shields*, the artist used pieces of Carol Shields' clothing, a vest and jean skirt, each with their many buttons, as the basis for her memorial to the writer.

Thus, like her symbols and artistic methods, the actual materials and objects Sabiston selects further blend the dichotomies of message and language—that unique visual language she continues to develop. Her 2009 symphony works, *Opus #1: In the Key of ?* and *Opus #2: In the Key of ?*, for instance, include keys taken from her vast collection of lost or discarded keys. The keys become the musicians, adding wit and a third dimension while simultaneously enhancing sensibilities or memories of the past to reveal the contradiction so frequent in contemporary times of being both "inside" and "locked out." The serious note in these works is her overarching question: what is society's direction? Is the artist evoking lost ways of life? How do changing policies and technologies affect the way we live? Sabiston admits to a desire to "hang on to the past" despite what she refers to as "frightening electronic changes."[9] These works bring to mind the comment by University of Toronto urban scholar John Lorinc:

> *In many ways, our intensely diverse cities have come to resemble grand orchestras, with countless performers playing a breathtaking array of instruments. We may all have a sense of harmony, the notes we'd like to play, and the solos we intend to perform. But unless we all find a way to agree on a score and then develop a vision of how to collaborate down there in the pit, there can only be noise.*[10]

Sabiston's working process—"pinning to stay," cutting, splicing and reversing strips—emphasizes the constant changes in political, economic and environmental directions. Her process and images together consistently raise the hard questions contemporary society faces: balancing the permanent and transitory, present conveniences with future responsibilities, and known and unknown.

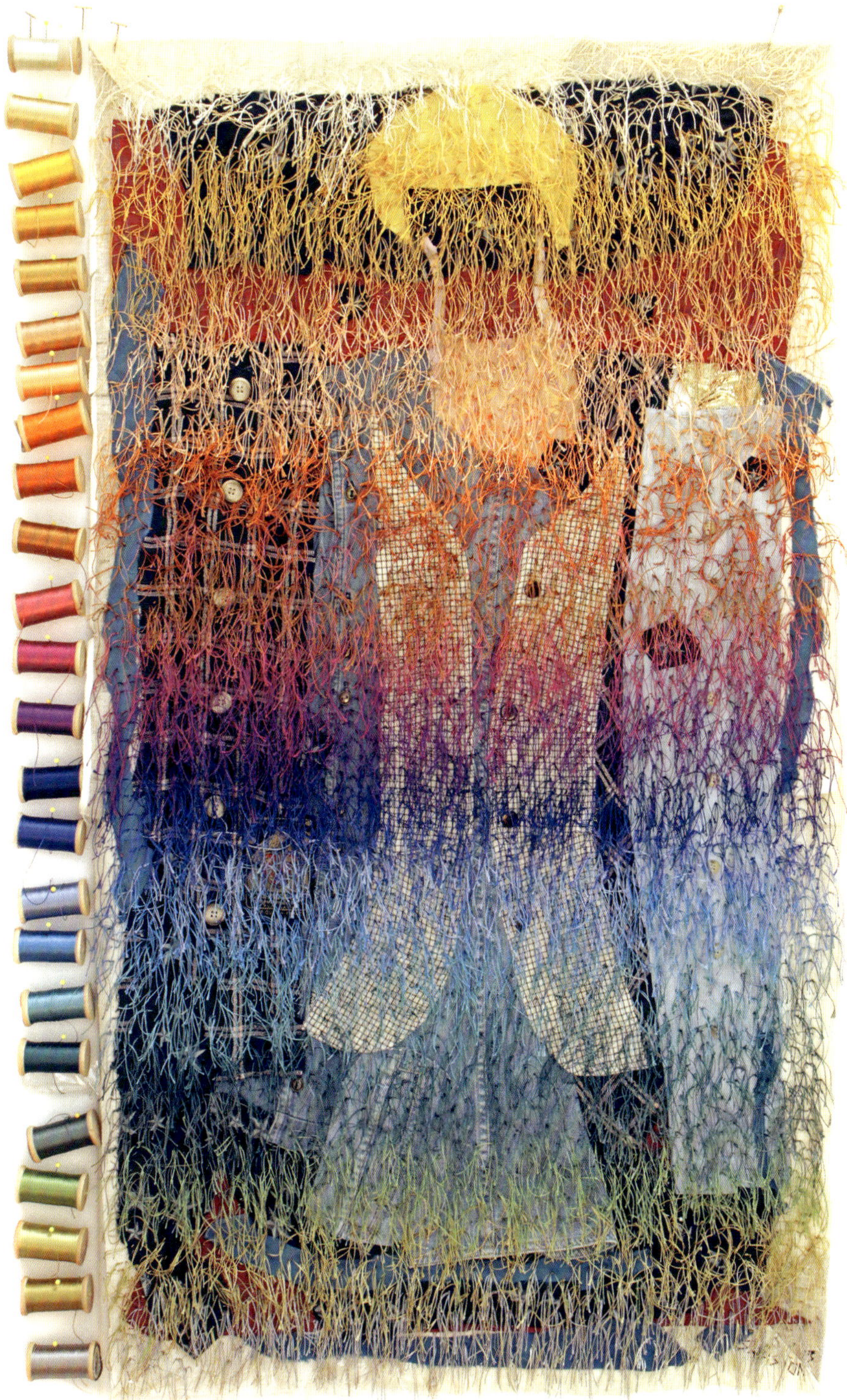

cat. 30 *Connecting Threads: Arc of Carol Shields*, 2013

Connecting Elements

From windows looking out to space or from space looking back to earth, I like to examine the concept of movement between near and far. I am compelled to look at the ways we travel around and through our environment in reality and in our imaginations. As a metaphor for silent travel, I have constructed three-dimensional sails, parachutes and flying carpets—all textile means of transportation.

—Carole Sabiston, in the Bronfman Collection Virtual Gallery at the Canadian Museum of Civilization

The connections between Sabiston's series, periods and iconography are strong. The phases in her work meld. Her wonderment at nature, the world and the universe in which we live underlies each phase, as does her overall concern at what we are doing to our environment. Sabiston's continuing exploration of the skies and space are reflected in her consistent imagery and her approaches to materials, colour and structure. The four elements—water, wind, earth and fire—feature in every decade, philosophically fusing her oeuvre, while permeating it with kinetic motion and rhythm. Water, for example, is the focal point in *Points of Ocean View* (1992); wind in *Sailing* (1982); earth in *Black's Island/Ice Lake Misted* (1990); and fire in *Royal Fireworks Suite* (1984).

Another constant is the way she blends past, present and future in a single work by incorporating both historical and contemporary references, as in *Flying into Delos* (1992) and *Everything Below: All of the Above* (2003). The latter includes imagery of fireworks, flying discs recalling old 78 records, and shapes made from black and white checkered strips, perhaps suggestive of the stock market's ticker tapes? The title, she notes, is taken from the essence of so "many business memos—'see below'—or media headlines—'none of the above.'"[11]

The symbolic meaning of lines is also constant throughout her body of work. The horizontal relates to the land; the vertical to growth; circular forms to the earth, its plants, seasons and seeds; and diagonals to wind, rain and clouds.[12] These meanings are especially evident in *Four Seasons Suite*, installed in Munro's Books, Victoria; *Flying into Delos;* and *Spatial Possibilities: Dissecting an Examination*. Further, the metaphors she uses for the ephemeral and for atmospheric fleeting moments, which recur in many series, consistently suggest fantasy, escape and freedom.

Sabiston's portrayal of place provides yet another connector underlying her entire body of work. This device defines her geographical and personal perceptions. Many compositions relate to specific places she has lived: "I've always lived on islands, and my work is a lot about changes in atmosphere, where the only constant is change; you always know that the horizon is there, but what goes on with the colours, back and forth, is always in flux."[13] *Points of Ocean View* and *Sailing* are prime examples.

Fly the Horizon (2009) and *Take Off: Point of Departure and Mode of Travel* (1987-1989) also demonstrate consistent characteristics in her work—the reality of island life coupled with fantasy, silent movement, space, the four elements and the juxtaposition of the macro and micro. Of *Take Off: Point of Departure and Mode of Travel,* the artist states:

> *This is a particular flight that I take very often as do many people who live in this region where we are either plowing across the water or flying above it. I chose this particular area because it is a direct area of transport. There is a carpet itself embedded into the surface of the earth. I have always had a great fascination with Kilims or rugs from the Orient, in the random patterns, each pattern peculiar to the weaver or region it has come from. I like to think this is a modern, contemporary carpet made of extraordinary and exotic fabrics far out of reality. The carpet itself is at the same time the earth and a carpet. It's an aerial view between Victoria on Vancouver Island, and Vancouver on the Mainland, flying over the Gulf Islands.*[14]

In the original installation of this large work, the earth, the floor piece, was supported by Plexiglas rods of graduated heights, suggesting the natural undulations in the land and the sense of the earth's carpet lifting off into space. The sky canopy, suspended from the ceiling, was made of layers of netting and gauze into which the artist incorporated a number of real and fantasy objects among the clouds:

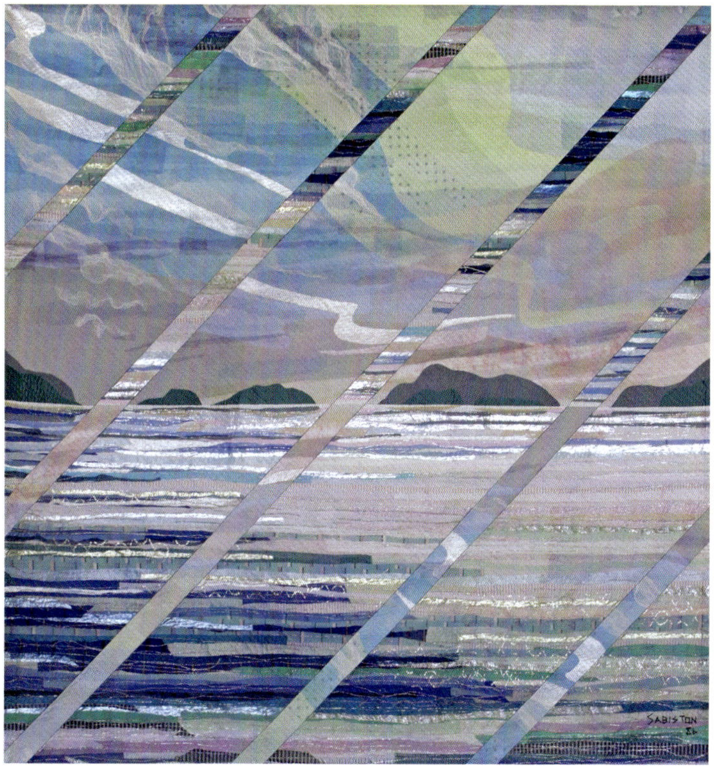

cat. 15
Islands in Colour II, 1986

> *Some of the details in the sky or in the atmosphere allude to things that are flying in present-day reality or imaginary. For instance, we have satellites, all kinds of planes, from helicopters to Twin Otters, to the Concorde. We have Superman, of course, and we have two gloves almost touching. This, perhaps, is a reference to Michelangelo's* The Creation of Man. *It's always that illusion [as we] look up at the sky and the clouds, and I always see gaps or dinosaurs, or a soup plate or whatever you want. It's all these illusions of things that fly up in the sky, and they are there.*[15]

That approach to depicting the sky is found in many works. In *The Flying Rondels at Dawn* (1987), the netting in the sky—the clouds—becomes flying,

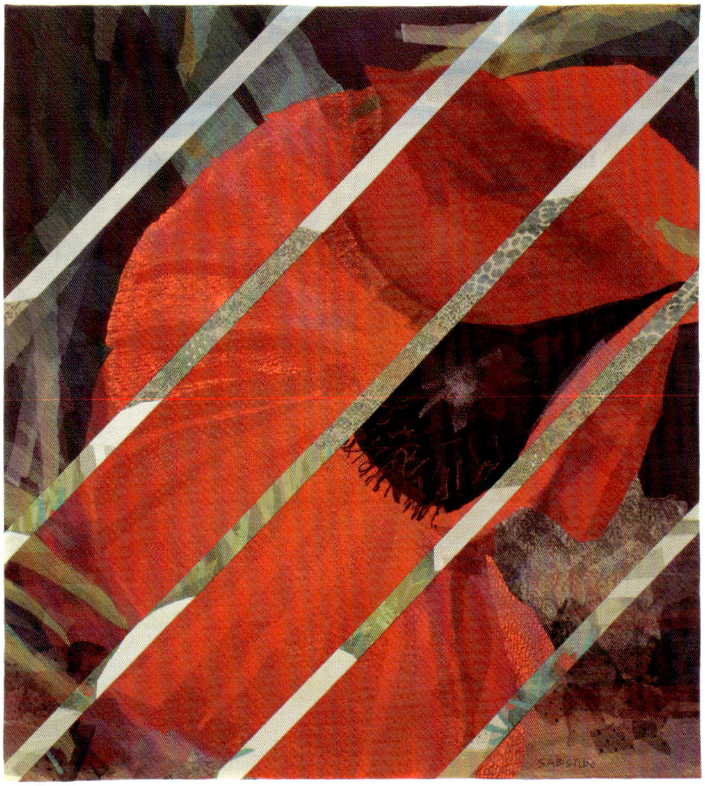

cat. 21
Flying into Delos (detail), 1992

floating, weightless figures drifting above the sea and islands.

Flying into Delos (1992), a four-panelled work, examines the near and the far, and changing perspectives and viewpoints, inspired in part by the invention of zoom lenses newly accessible to all. The far left-hand panel is the view as one approaches the island of Delos and depicts reflections on the Mediterranean and clouds moving across the sky. The next panel focuses on the island's landscape—the ruins and dry vegetation. As the eye moves further right, one sees a close-up of remaining fragments of marble columns and stones, vermillion poppies nestled between them. The last panel zooms in on only one poppy blossom, blown up many times larger than life, filling the entire six-foot-square panel. Filled with rich colour, Sabiston's characteristic spliced diagonals are re-inserted into the work in reverse—the diagonals in one panel are those cut from another, thus changing the colour dynamic within each panel and forming a zigzag pattern across all four panels. These lineal combinations purposely set up symbolic tensions, contrasting the fluidity of nature with the constructivist composition. The linear tension and thrust, coupled with the fragmented imagery, are integral to her message. Taking us back in time, the artist articulated her goals for this work:

> *I wanted the idea of actually flying into history. Delos was the spiritual home of the ancient Greeks. It's a very small island, and at one time it was a sacred city. Giving birth there was forbidden; women had to leave during their menses; no one could be ill. Now it's peace and ruins. The history is so evocative, it's bouncing all over your skin. It was the most magical experience. That stayed with me, and a few years later I did the work.*[16]

Sabiston's definitions of common words are equally illuminating. She refers to the movement of the sea as "a liquid atmosphere"; the sky as "a translucent force"; and island life as "rootlessness" or a "floating sense."[17] These ephemeral shifts of moods and ever-changing atmospheres play on the horizon lines through her deft layering of opaque and translucent materials. She uses her textiles as a painter uses paint, and the nettings and sheers evoke tonalities, much as glazes do for the potter.

Moving Into the Here and on to the Beyond

I have eschewed conventional art history and traditional modes of art making, preferring to find new ways to explore issues, many being offbeat when I first portrayed them.

—Carole Sabiston, in conversation with Patricia Bovey (August 7, 2013)

Sabiston's work psychologically, philosophically and metaphorically is both ahead of, and within, her own time. Her concern about our poor treatment of the environment and lack of protection of rare species is paramount. In *Flying Rufus* (2009), the hummingbird image, much larger than life, draws attention to the vulnerabilities of fragile species while linking flight in nature to her images of magical flight. Vertical strips of various textured materials across the lower picture plane, with a label reading *FLAX*, represent the grasses and vegetation. At both edges of the "grasses" there are cards of thread samples, suggesting continuing connections beyond the frame to the past and to the future. Iridescent materials form the hummingbird itself. The eye and parts of the upper wing are from the eighteenth-century Spanish cope used in *Reredos*. The upper wing is a canvas with pencil drawing from the original maquette for *Take Off: Point of Departure and Mode of Travel*. The artist notes: "It [*Take Off*] flies again!"[18] Clouds are of cheesecloth, and the petals are details cut from hundred-year-old dresses and fabrics that the artist found in a family trunk. Enhancing the fragility of the subject itself, everything in *Flying Rufus* is held in place by glass, not overstitching. Sabiston's concern is for the future of that minute species, which is so important to the natural ecology of the world. In works like this, the artist's sense of place and history takes her from "here," her own garden, "on to the beyond" in both thought and time.

Spatial Possibilities Series, exhibited at the 1988 Calgary Olympics, like *Take Off: Point of Departure and Mode of Travel*, marks another way in which Sabiston is "ahead of her time." These works were created only a few years after Marc Garneau became the first Canadian in space in 1984. Even then, Sabiston was concerned about the increasing amounts of debris from space missions, and about the presumption that the debris would orbit the earth in perpetuity. Sabiston's works dealing with these issues were presented in several Canadian centres when Roberta Bondar became the first Canadian woman in space. Most recently, just months before the current exhibition, Chris Hadfield returned from his epic journey and command of the International Space Station. As international space explorations, and concerns over accumulating amounts of junk in outer space, accelerate, these textile assemblages continue to be as relevant today as they were at the time of their creation. Given today's escalating global environmental crises, Sabiston's clairvoyance in exposing these problems through her visual explorations as early as the 1980s and 1990s is poignant. She talks nostalgically of seeing Sputnik,

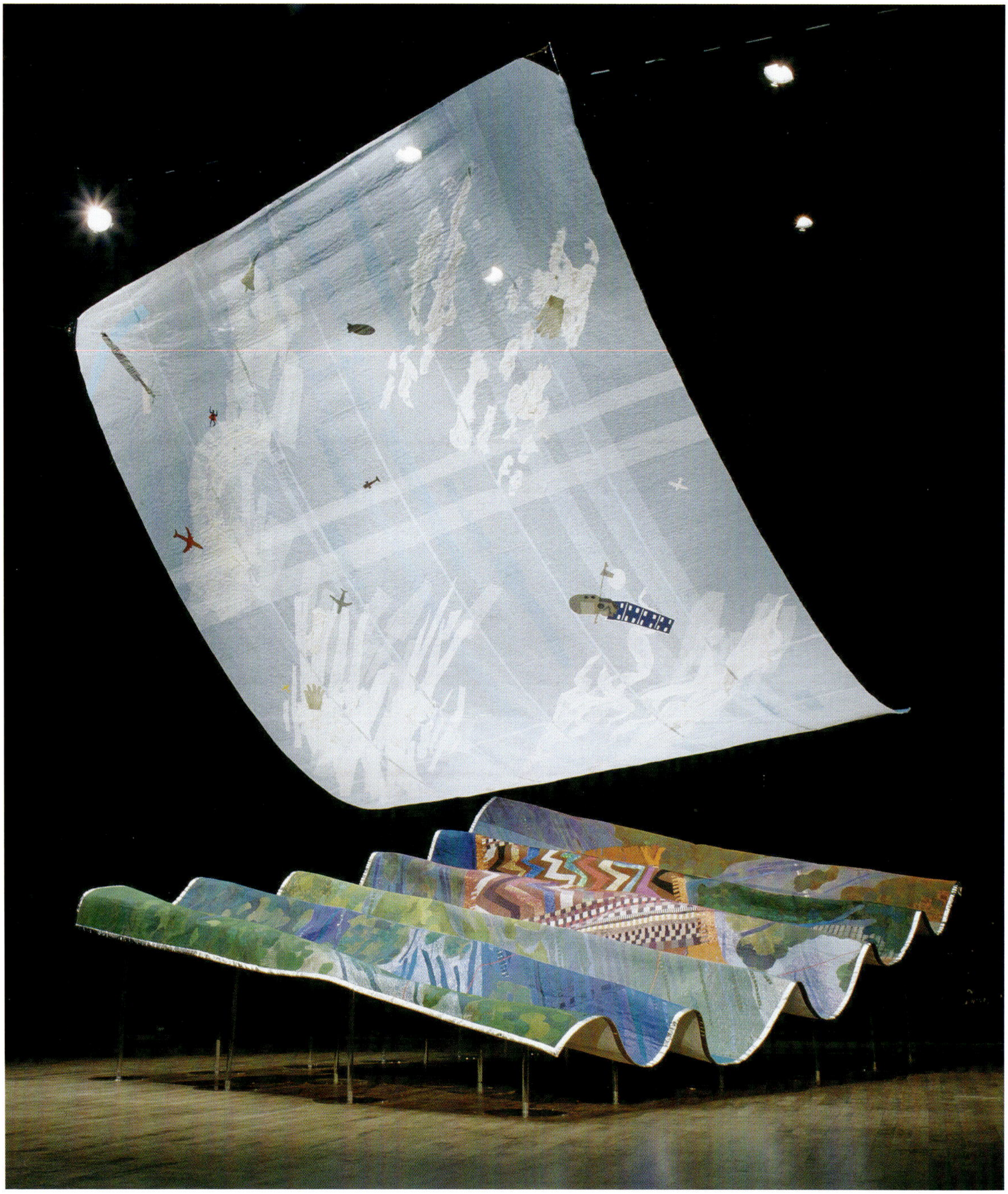

Take Off: Point of Departure and Mode of Travel, 1987–1989, textile assemblage installation, 365.76 x 365.76 x 365.76cm

launched in 1957, crossing the skies as she and her parents watched from their Victoria porch—sparking her ongoing interest in space, which continues these many years later. Of space debris, Sabiston has said:

> *The Flying Carpet, or as we fondly call it, the Magic Carpet, evoked the memory of childhood fairytales. You know, all children have ways of going on their magic carpets and finding their fantasies in the world. I've always wondered, ever since childhood, whatever happened to all those flying carpets from Persia. There must have been thousands that must have escaped, so I presume they are up there orbiting the earth along with the 7000 pieces of space debris that the space programme has sent up.*[19]

In May 2013, the European Space Agency estimated that 29,000 pieces of space debris were orbiting the world, 17,000 of which were being tracked daily.[20]

Sabiston has always been interested in the human dimension, but her depiction of actual figures is infrequent. In *Spatial Possibilities Series: Individual Take Off* (1988), however, while continuing her theme of here to beyond, she did include human silhouettes, returning to imagery not seen in her work since the 1960s. Here, "tiny figures dangle from parachute threads as they fly through the air...I was quite excited about this one and probably will be getting back into figurative work.'"[21] Her *Flying Revolution Quartet* (1993) also includes flying figures circling the globe, some flying towards the earth, some away, and some around it, just as space debris does. Was she forecasting trips to Mars? In *Flying Revolution Quartet*, the four square sections, blue, red, orange and green, each have their own energy, and the changing moods of the earth, the island, shift from one quadrant to the next.

The changes of perception, perspective, distance and space, so central to Sabiston's work, are accentuated by her fusing the macro and micro, and the far and near, in every work. Never compromising the "big picture," she depicts minute details of location, a moment or her particular concern. The *Sailing* series of the early 1980s was her first serious exploration of wind and movement on water. Each sail proffers views of the waters around Victoria—both sides of each sail afford a different vista, yet all have a constant horizon line. The rocks anchoring the sails, each weighing seventy-five pounds, were collected from Vancouver Island beaches. Viewers create movement among the sails as they walk through the installation.

Flying explores silent motion through space. Flight and movement in space have always intrigued Sabiston, and the magic carpet became her symbol. Through its many iterations—large and small, embedded in the landscape, as the earth itself, flying through the universe singly or in squadrons, or captured in pickle jars—Sabiston's magic carpet also references diverse world cultures. Her preoccupation with silent travel

> *reflects a dynamic energy consistent with voyages through time and space...She challenges herself to make visible the highly predicable movement of planets, the random movement of the stuff we have discarded*

in space and the elusive movement of the wind. She sees the tension in the motion and constants of the natural worlds, citing for example the horizon, the "imperceptible line between ever-changing constants of sky and sea; limitless, infinite." [22]

Whether depicting specific places close to home, in the Gulf Islands, or as far away as Greece or the Silk Road in China and Tibet, her juxtapositions of real and imaginary images, factual and mythical, magnify her lasting message of environmental concern.

Sabiston often speaks of the inherent contrasts of meaning in her materials, and her interest in history resurfaces:

> *An ongoing interest for me...is fabric and how it is used in flight. It works on a silent theory where there are no engines involved. So I have done the series starting with the parachute, then going into sails, and now the flying carpet which has come in many forms...*
>
> *I'm really concerned and fascinated with the idea of fabric which has no energy or life-force while it is bundled up, such as a parachute would be, or when sails are furled, or when a flying carpet is rolled up. But as soon as it is exposed to the air, the atmosphere, and the wind it takes on an enormous power of its own and can surge all around the world. This has been going on through the history of many civilizations, and is one of the earliest inventions. I'm trying to illustrate the dichotomies between the useless bundled fabric and the open fabric.*[23]

Sabiston's work does not portray only those voyages through and over the landscape. She has also created works that are psychological "inscapes" or biographical portraits. She feels *Connecting Threads: Arc of Carol Shields*, a recent portrait "inscape," may be "the deepest personal work I have ever done."[24] Sabiston's title for this work continues the theme of the three *Dropped Threads* anthologies edited by Carol Shields and Marjorie Anderson. Changing early iterations of *Connecting Threads: Arc of Carol Shields* had been pinned to Sabiston's studio wall as the work evolved over time. Spools of antique French silk threads, symbolizing Shields' love of France, are framed along the left side of the work. Veiling the ghost-like background image of the author are two-inch loose thread ends from Sabiston's hand-done traditional tailor's tacks. Shields' image was created from her own clothes and buttons. The loose silk threads and spools collectively reference the myriad ideas, connections and stories of the author. Colour moves in tone through the composition, from light to dark, top to bottom, mirroring Shields' sense of the arc of life.

Another 2013 work, *Pockets for Men's Trousers*, conjectures about the mysteries and meanings of trouser pockets, where they went and what they carried. The pockets in the work, from business suits, dress pants and casual wear, were interior pockets, sewn inside the trousers. Each had its own architecture, and, as the artist states, the making of each pocket was outsourced and it was then incorporated into the original garment. Pockets evoke both outside and inside worlds; they traverse the world but contain what the world cannot perceive. Everyone has pockets in which to carry personal private objects, notes, lists or keys, and

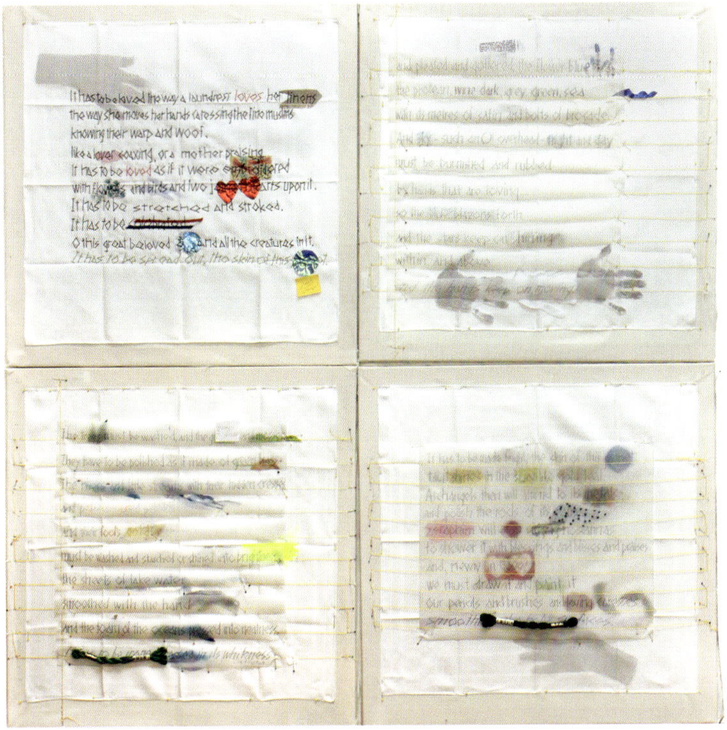

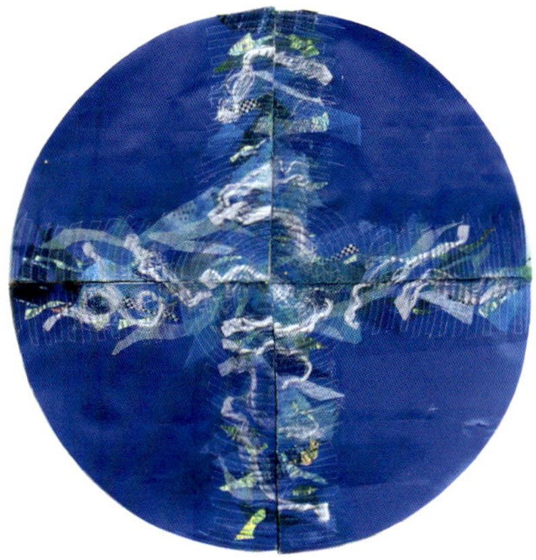

cat. 31
Planet Earth: After P. K. Page, (work in progress), 2013

no one other than the carrier knows what is "in" the pocket. This work has many pockets affixed over Sabiston's father's butcher aprons, overlapping each other like shingles on a roof. Was this layering a protective, purposeful application to guard the secrets within the pockets? Placed over the entire piece is a Plexiglas panel with text, in red, suggestive of signs in a butcher shop. The text is a true 1935 story involving the artist's father, George Slater, then a butcher on Portobello Road in London. He had a customer who came to the shop daily and would hand him a bit of paper with her one want noted. He always filled her order. After some time he gave her a note in return, asking what she, a deaf-mute, did for a living: "I make pockets for men's trousers."[25] The power of the story and the image of this tiny woman, all alone, making these carriers of private lives, has haunted the artist for years. Her own human compassion is paramount in this multi-layered psychological portrayal of both the butcher and the lady.

P.K. Page, a distinguished Canadian poet, is another friend, whose poem "Planet Earth" is the focus of Sabiston's 2013 piece of the same title, created with the author's permission. This iconic poem has been used internationally as the rallying cry for Earth Day. Sabiston was drawn to Page's imagery of the earth's skin as textiles, to be washed, ironed and pleated. Many years earlier, Sabiston had done a sketch of *Earth's Skin*, which later became the embryo of her larger aerial pieces. In *Planet Earth: After P. K. Page*, she stitched the four stanzas of the poem onto the fine linen napkins of her mother-in-law's trousseau, each section in its own quadrant. Sabiston collaged images, such as a star from the eighteenth-century cope and a flower from another heritage textile, to replace specific words. Tying the four quadrants together is an image of earth from space. One can see the connections with many of Sabiston's prior works—the use of text, old and new materials, views from outer space and the four-part structure.

Impacts Spanning Canada

> *I find collaborations with architects, designers, actors, musicians, authors, directors and set designers stimulating and energizing. My visual transformations are often through such collaborations.*
>
> —Carole Sabiston, in conversation with Patricia Bovey (June 7, 2013)

Public and corporate commissions for Carole Sabiston have come from all over Canada, some recommended by her Toronto agents, Jeanne Parkin and Jane Zeidler. Allan Edwards, then a New York designer, sparked this interest when he saw her work in the late 1960s and asked if she could, or would, do larger pieces. With that overture, she did! Sabiston also submitted proposals to public competitions of interest to her, particularly those allowing one-on-one creative engagement with the architect, and those that described the site and project standards in a way that respected the artist and work. The siting of the piece was particularly important to Sabiston, as was the commission's articulated goal, which had to resonate with her own philosophy. Her commissioned works were often monumental in scale, embodying the kinetic movement and multiple reflections Sabiston readily portrayed as she captured the illusive. She would often see these large commissions for the first time when they were installed, as her studio was too small to hang more than a few of the many panels at one time.

She recalls the commission for the Saanich Police and Fire Building (1997) as a particularly rewarding and compelling challenge and a truly collaborative and enjoyable project. She was able to develop the work with the architect, David Hambleton, and to be part of the decisions about the interior finishes where her piece was installed. *Locate* (1997), an octapytch or eight-panelled assemblage, represents the four locations of fire and police buildings in Saanich. For the artist, the four wheels are also symbolic of these vehicles being in the public service. The local landscape is featured, and the hubs of each station radiate across the fields and roads of the area.

Ottawa City Hall has another commission celebrating municipal histories and settings, *Rivers Reflecting Seasons* (1990). An eleven-panelled work, it reflects the Ottawa, Rideau and Gatineau Rivers, and each panel represents one former municipality, now all united as the Capital Regional District. Full of energy, patterns of fields and movement of water, silver and gold materials reflect the seasons—the water, ice, snow and the light of the landscape.

An unexpected private commission came from British author P.D. James for the curved staircase wall in her sixteenth-century Southwold home in Suffolk. She commissioned it for her own eightieth birthday, and according to her granddaughter it is "the family's favourite piece."[26] James herself

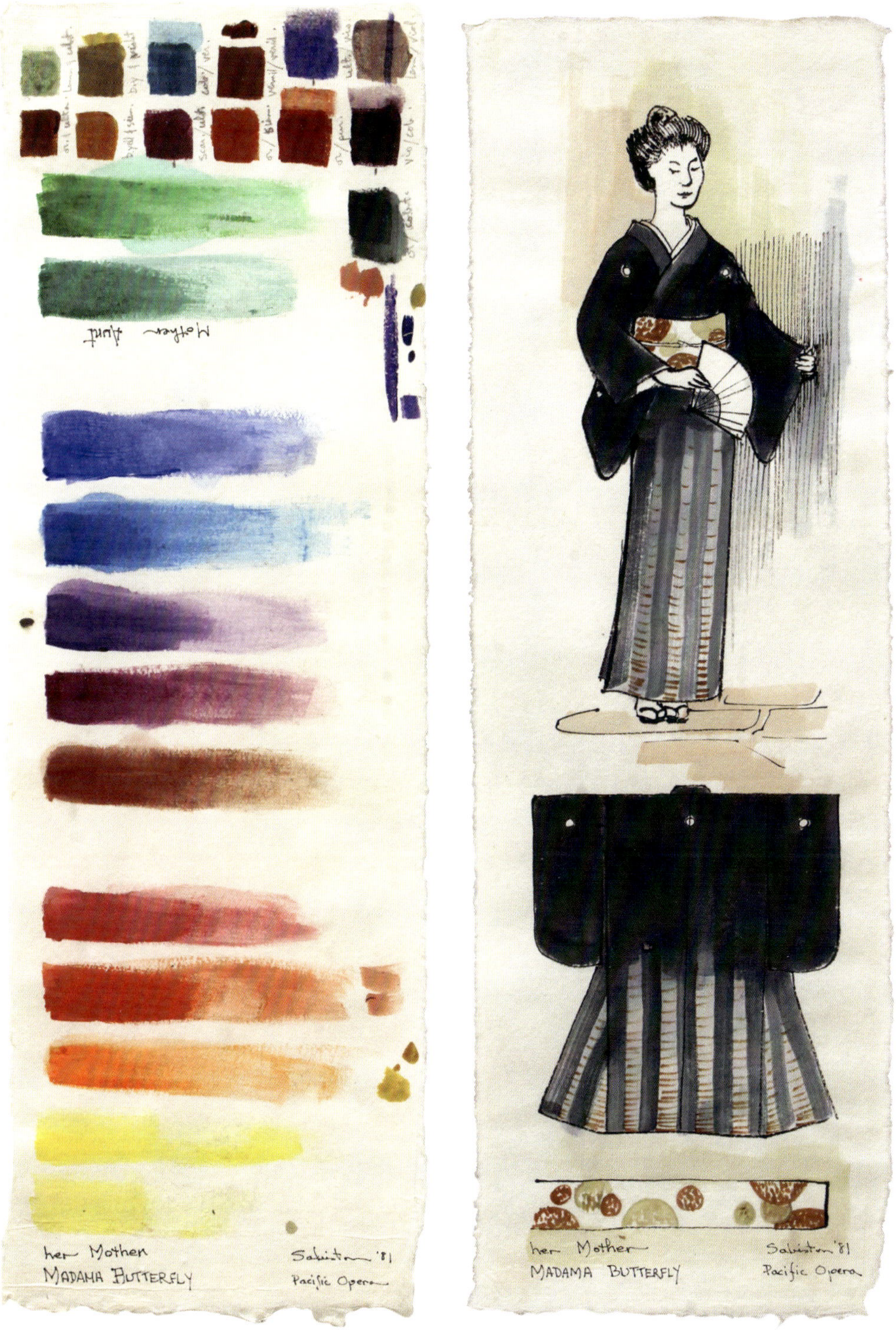

cat. 33, 34 *Working Sketches: Madama Butterfly*, 1981

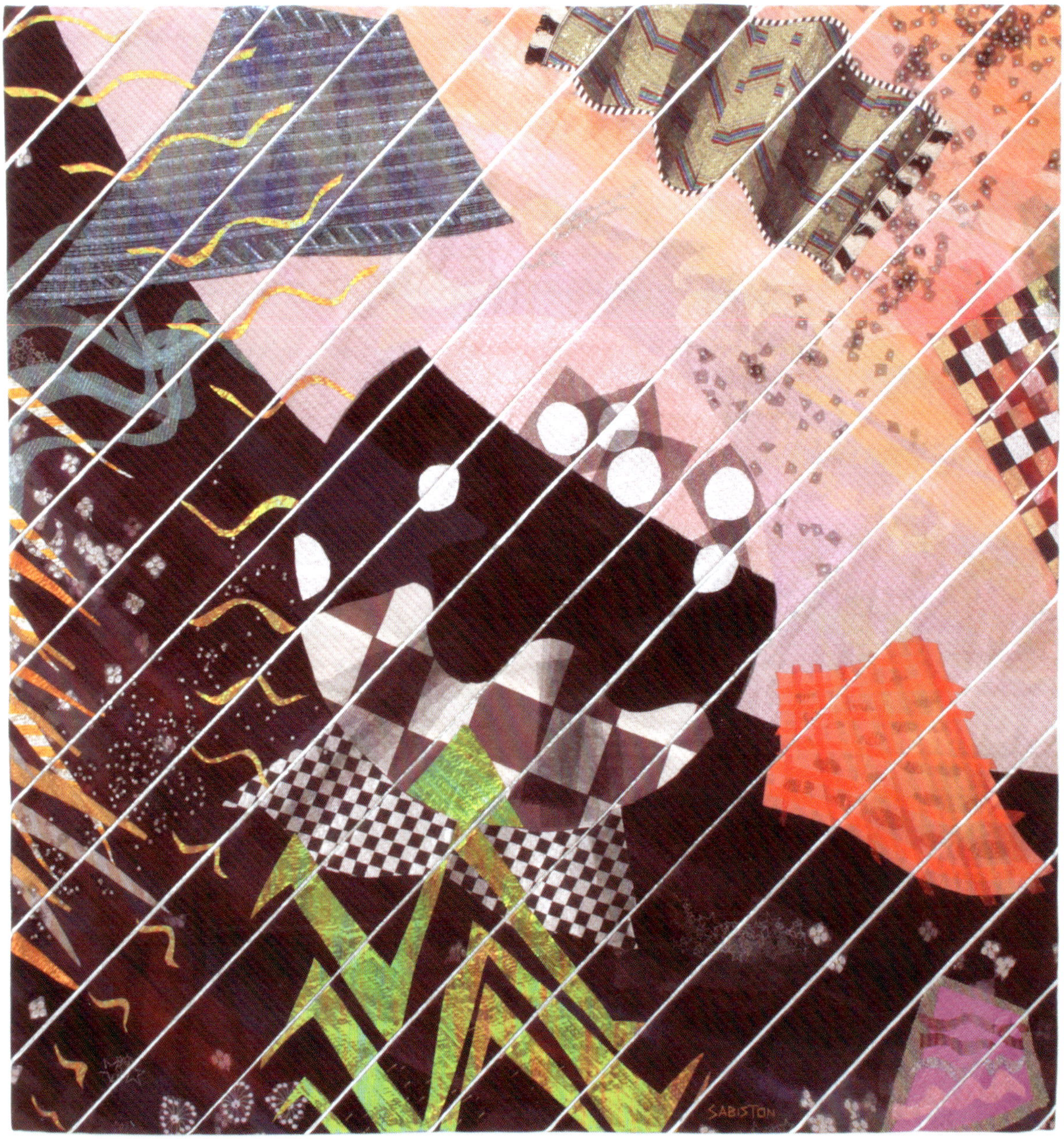

cat. 16 *Spatial Possibilities: Dissecting an Examination*, 1987 & 1994

commented in a note of thanks to the artist that this is her "favourite work with its scudding clouds over the lurid sky."[27] Sabiston travelled to the UK and spent time in Southwold, walking the beaches and marshes, and visiting churches with James in order to gain a sense of James' country life. They watched ballets and mysteries together, all of which gave the artist ideas for the ensuing work. Five feet wide and six feet high, the final piece includes images from the area collaged into the textile assemblage, with titles of the author's many books embroidered throughout the bulrushes. Sabiston worked quickly on this commission and sent James preliminary drawings shortly after her memorable visit. In Sabiston's typical fashion, she included a portfolio of progress photographs and sketches with the finished piece.

I had the privilege of being invited to Sabiston's studio on many occasions to see works the night before shipping. These were exciting moments, celebrating the completion of a major work and the start of its journey and future public impact. Public art such as Sabiston's unquestionably creates community pride. Recent research has also shown that public art reduces crime and enhances both workplaces and public gathering spaces.

Despite the exhilaration of securing, creating and installing her many commissions and public art contracts, there were disappointments. Some works have mysteriously disappeared—removed or destroyed without her knowledge. We can only presume that, in the wake of corporate mergers and sales, new owners were unaware of the protocols, the contractual agreements with the artist or the obligation to consult her. In 1986, for instance, the developer Zwig commissioned three large works—*Spatial Possibilities: the Ruby Red Planet, Spatial Possibilities; the Harvest Gold Planet* and *Spatial Possibilities: the Blush Pink Planet*—for the office building at 4 King Street West, Toronto. This was a major installation that garnered significant acclaim and was "all about silent travel, fantasy and an escape."[28] Again we see space debris and the profile of planet earth below. The whole installation was removed by new building owners and found later, crumpled in a corner. Two pieces had been destroyed and the third stolen. This is, unquestionably, a loss to Canadian art and the public. There have, however, been other instances of mergers and corporate buy-outs where the artist has been contacted, and works no longer wanted have been donated to public galleries or university collections.

In addition to her studio work and commissions, Sabiston has done set and costume designs for theatre and opera. Victoria's Kaleidoscope Theatre and the Victoria Symphony inaugurated travelling school productions in the 1980s, which Sabiston was very involved with, including *Kaleidophonics.* Pacific Opera projects, which included costumes for *The Magic Flute* and *Madama Butterfly,* were collaborative engagements as stimulating as the alliances with architects. Her theatre work connected philosophically to all her work, full of movement, colour, spontaneity and the ephemeral. Conscious of the "act" of installing pieces, the ability to fold, roll or easily move the art was paramount and part of the overall challenge.

Always a natural teacher, Sabiston's teaching career began when she was nineteen years old and continued until she took a leave of absence in 1973 to focus on studio work and found she could live on

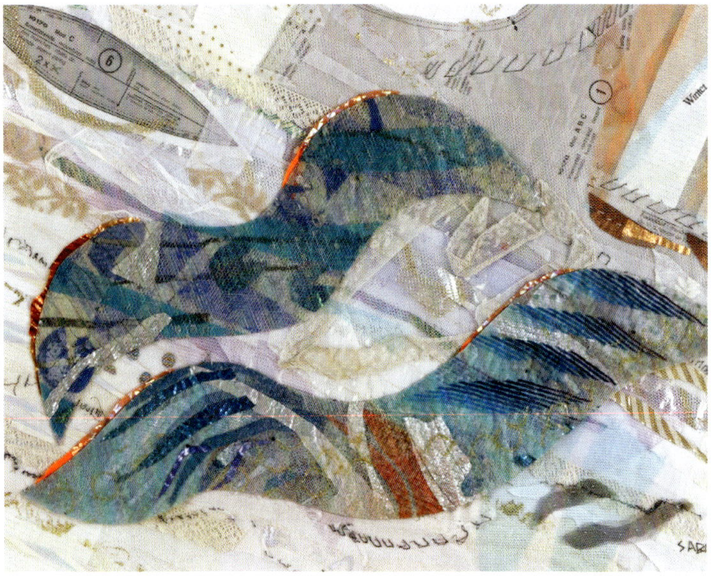

cat. 27
Flight Patterns
(detail), 2009

commissions and her art. Whether in the classroom or, subsequently, working with students on special projects, she always drew from her inventive insights, simultaneously engaging her students and infecting her own work with new energy.

This frequent and intrepid traveller has visited many parts of the world—the first major trip being to Spain in 1969. She has continued to travel ever since, seeking new places, experiences and both old and new forms of visual expression. The United Kingdom, Eastern and Western Europe, Japan, China, Tibet and the United States have all been on her radar screen. All have played a significant role in her art. Connections with colleague artists have been important, the exchange of ideas with peers as revealing as her exchanges with students. It is not a surprise that this artist has been an active member of the Royal Canadian Academy of Arts and of Victoria's Limner Society of Artists. Camaraderie, shared creative experiences and varied exhibition opportunities have all fed the work and career of Carole Sabiston.

Intersections? Synchronicities? Crosswinds? Linkages? Overlappings? Juxtapositions? Any of these words convey Sabiston's overall objective. Her philosophy and approach are unique, unquestionably interwoven throughout her inventive visual vocabulary, just as the themes she has explored over the decades intersect and build on each other. Throughout her work she always questions and reflects current issues—environmental, social and cultural. Reflecting the past while presenting warnings for the future, she does so with joy, humour, warmth, immediacy and accessibility. Her messages of "here to there," physical and psychological, are highlighted by her superimpositions of formal diagonal grids over the fluidity of veils of clouds and moods. That is as she lives her life—a strong ethic and routine coupled with a freedom and flexibility, allowing her to engage in new experiences at home and abroad and with family and friends. Her many awards signal the esteem in which she is held. She, in turn, heralds the compelling need for humanity to understand and preserve our universe, our communities and our own individual sensibilities.

The work of Carole Sabiston is indeed *Everything Below All of the Above*.

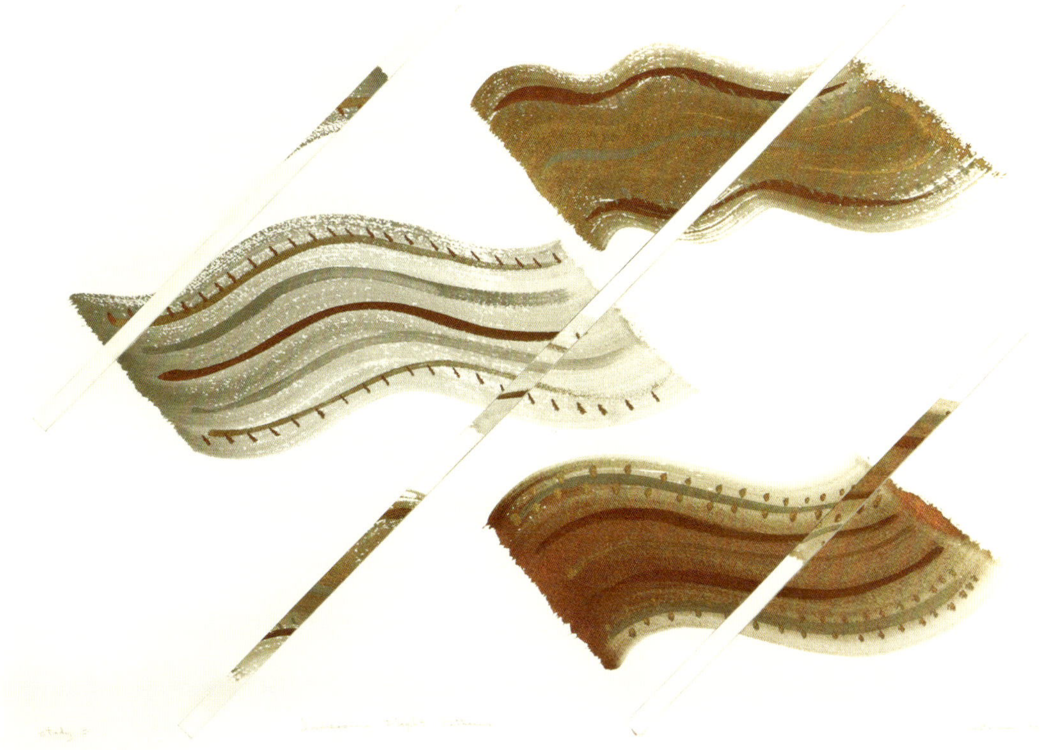

cat. 38
Flying Carpets Study #3, 1990

Endnotes

1. Carole Sabiston in conversation with Patricia Bovey, December 21, 2012.
2. Marie Shaw-Rimmington, quoted by Pam Bristol, "Carole Sabiston 1987 Bronfman Winner," *Ontario Craft* (Winter 1987): 18.
3. Carole Sabiston in conversation with Patricia Bovey, June 7, 2013.
4. P.K. Page, in *Art on Video: The Art of Carole Sabiston* (Art Gallery of Greater Victoria, 1990), Videocassette.
5. Quoted in Barbara Lee Smith, *Celebrating the Stitch: Contemporary Embroidery of North America* (Taunton Press, 1991), 10.
6. Smith, *Celebrating the Stitch*, 10.
7. Ibid., 12.
8. Ibid., 13.
9. Carole Sabiston in conversation with Patricia Bovey, June 7, 2013.
10. John Lorinc, *The New City: How the Crisis in Canada's Urban Centres Is Reshaping the Nation* (Penguin Canada, 2006), 329.
11. Carole Sabiston in conversation with Patricia Bovey, June 7, 2013.
12. Carole Sabiston in conversation with Patricia Bovey, July 1988; reflected also in several of her Artist's Statements.
13. Carole Sabiston interview with Patricia Bovey, July 1988; quoted in Patricia Bovey, *Carole Sabiston: Flying* (Art Gallery of Greater Victoria, 1990), 8.
14. Quoted in Patricia Bovey, "Carole Sabiston: The Artist's Reflections on 'Flying' and 'Take Off: Point of Departure and Mode of Travel,'" *InSight: A Magazine about Contemporary Art* (Summer, 1990): 8.
15. Ibid.
16. Carole Sabiston in conversation with Patricia Bovey, July 1988.
17. Carole Sabiston in conversation with Patricia Bovey, December 21, 2012.
18. Carole Sabiston in conversation with Patricia Bovey, May 23, 2013.
19. Quoted in Bovey, "Carole Sabiston: The Artist's Reflections," 7.
20. Jason Dorrier, "Orbital Trash a Problem with No Immediate Solution," Singularity Hub website, May 23, 2013 (http://singularityhub.com/2013/05/23/orbital-trash-a-problem-with-no-immediate-solution-growing-exponentially/).
21. Bristol, "Carole Sabiston 1987 Bronfman Winner," 18.
22. Smith, *Celebrating the Stitch*, 8.
23. Quoted in Bovey, "Carole Sabiston: The Artist's Reflections," 8.
24. Carole Sabiston in conversation with Patricia Bovey, June 7, 2013.
25. Carole Sabiston in conversation with Patricia Bovey, May 23, 2013.
26. P.D. James' granddaughter, Beatrice Grove, in conversation with Patricia Bovey, July 2010.
27. Carole Sabiston in conversation with Patricia Bovey, December 21, 2012.
28. Carole Sabiston as quoted by Bristol in "Carole Sabiston 1987 Bronfman Winner," 17.

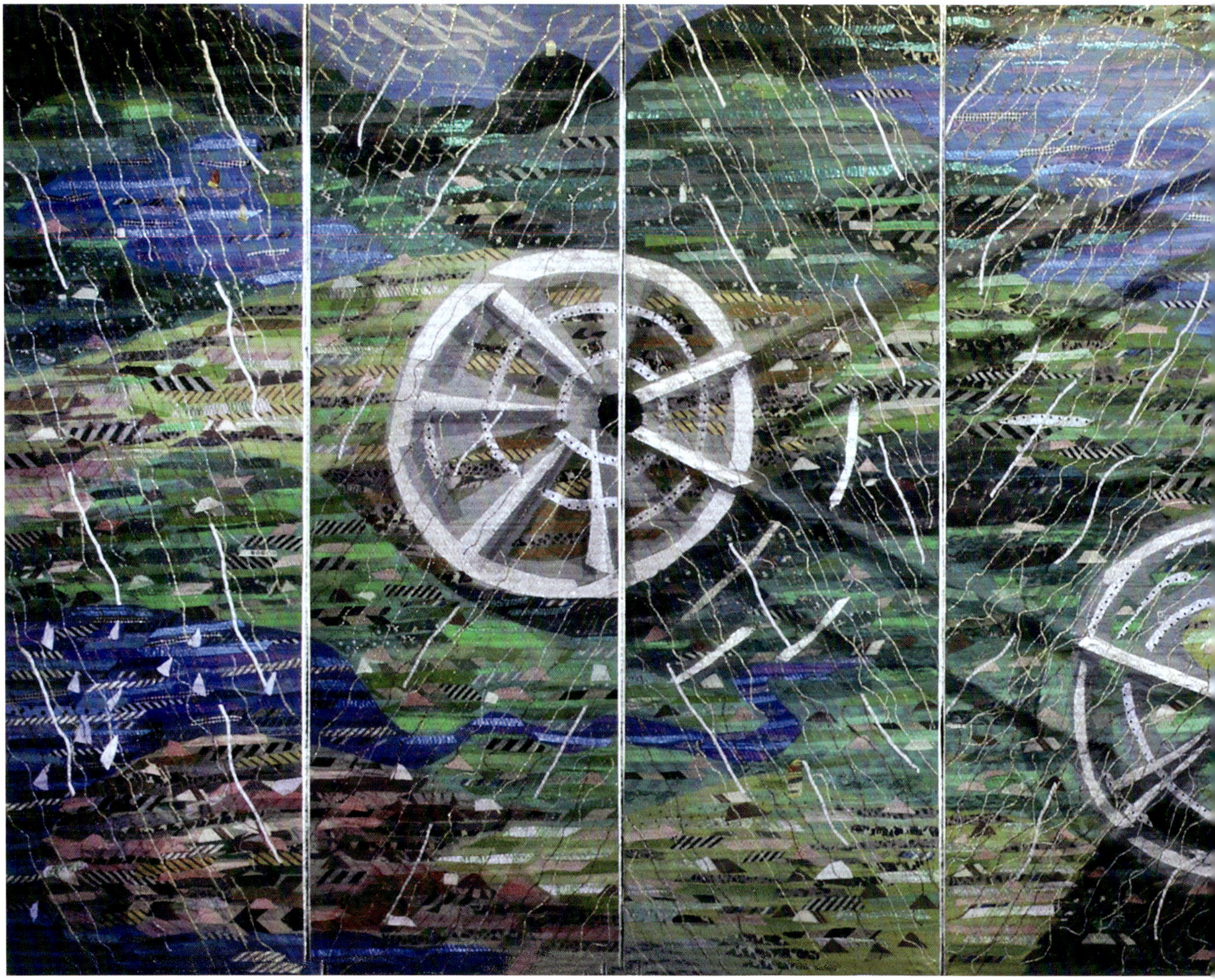

Locate, 1997, textile assemblage, 182 x 487.7cm, Saanich Police and Fire Building

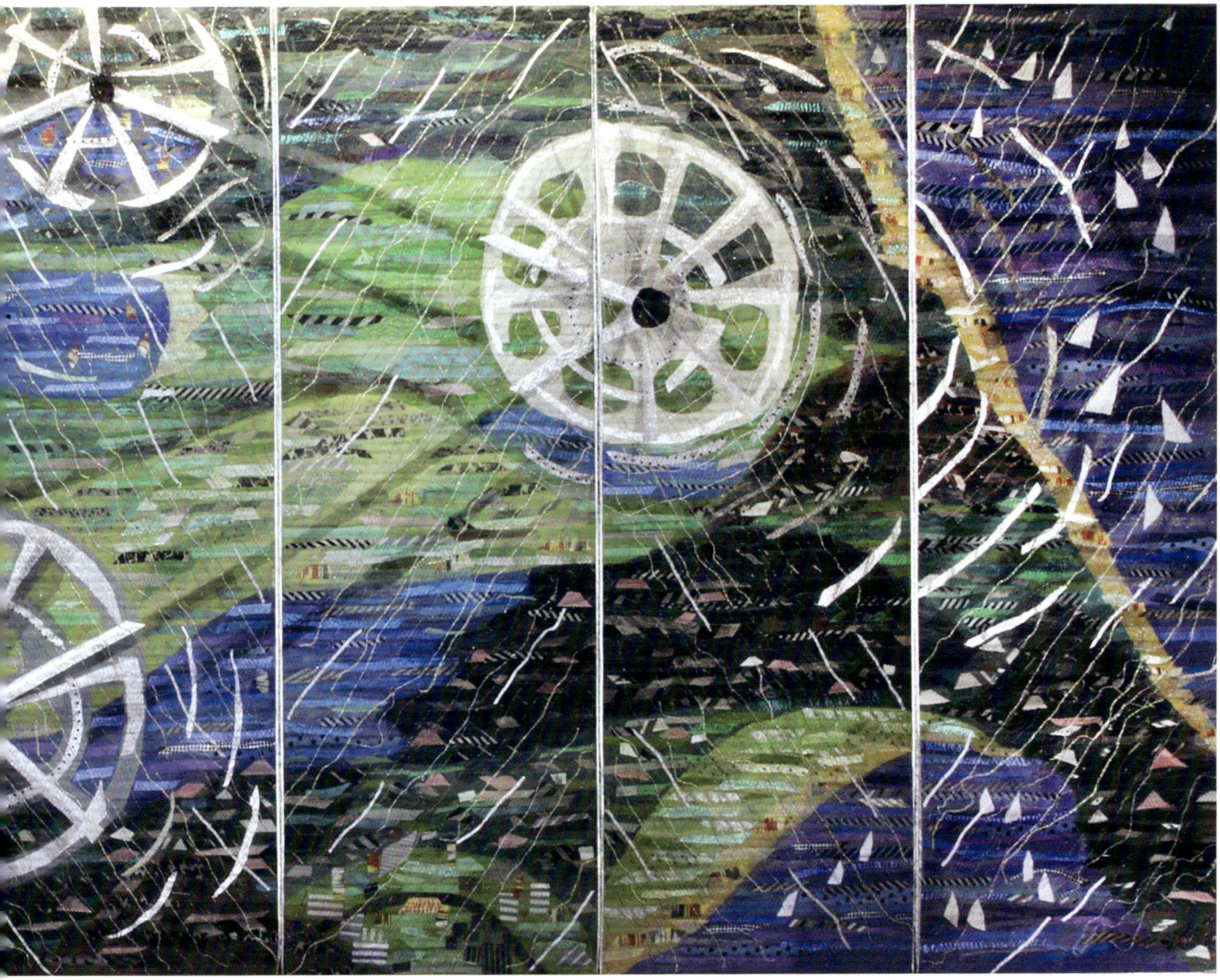

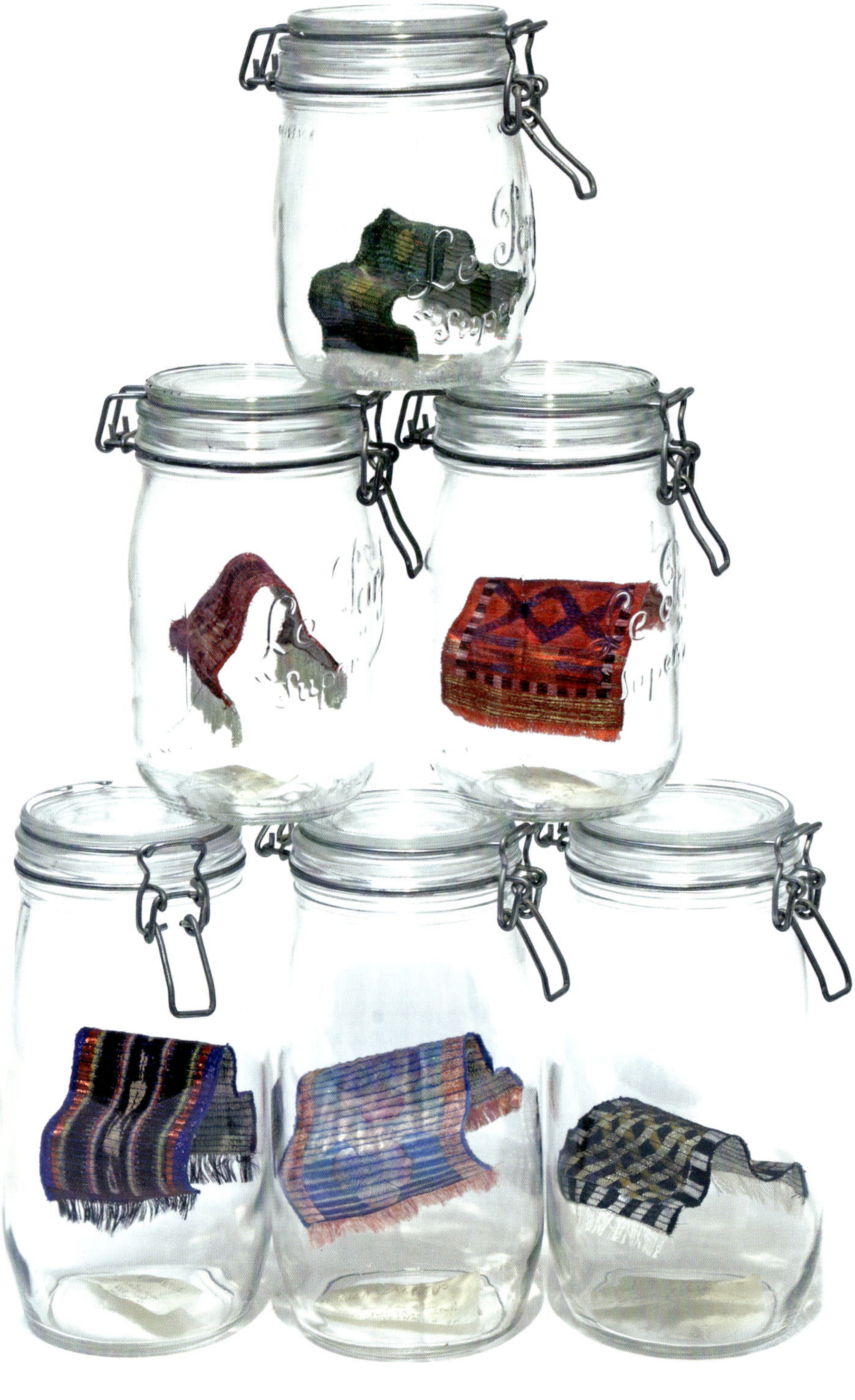

MICHELLE JACQUES

Connecting Threads: Placing Carole Sabiston in Art History

When Carole Sabiston began her professional career in the 1960s, it was as a painter. However, she found herself searching for a new artistic language that would allow her to achieve the effects of light, movement and texture that she aspired to express in her work. Sabiston had always been drawn to fabric, so she turned to textile art as a medium that could afford a vocabulary with enough range to achieve the complexity of composition and concern that she sought to convey. Variously layering, cutting, and piecing back together fabric of different colours, surfaces and translucencies with a method that merges aspects of collage, assemblage, quilting and appliqué, Sabiston creates murals, wall hangings, suspended sculptures and tapestries, sometimes as stand-alone objects, and often as site-specific undertakings that are deliberately conceived to enhance a particular site.

Sabiston is now internationally recognized for her textile works. They are created from fabrics, both new and salvaged; threads and yarns; rope, ribbons, nettings, buttons and other notions; and labels removed from their garments, as well as from things that are less inclined to be associated with textile art: paint, ink, plastic, metal, paper, photographs, even rocks. Her earliest textile works date from the mid-1960s; her embrace of the new medium came at a time when many women artists had turned to craft and the decorative arts as a feminist strategy. "Women's work"—quilting, embroidery, sewing, needlework, china painting—had been deemed a lesser category of art precisely because of its association with the feminine and the domestic sphere.

cat. 22
Magicus Carpetus: Squadron – Preserving a Flying Tradition, 1992

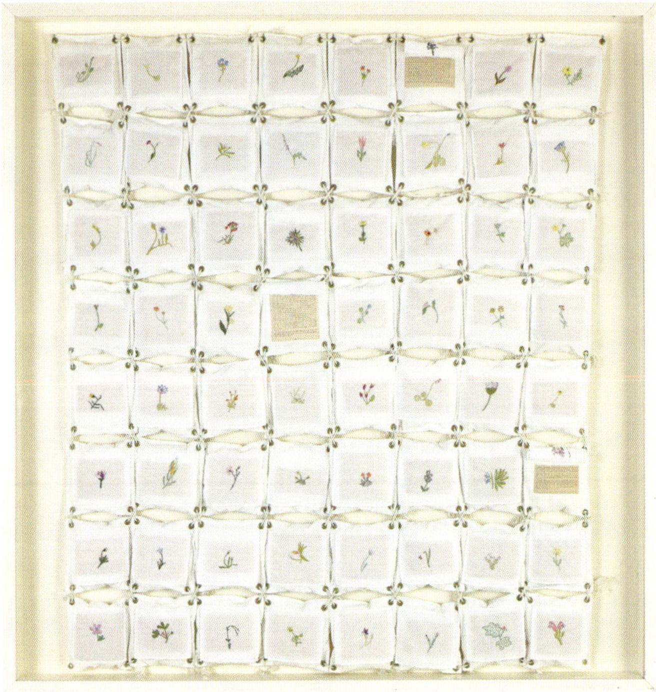

Joyce Wieland, *The Water Quilt*, 1970/71, fabric, embroidery thread, thread, metal grommets, braided rope, ink on fabric; Collection of Art Gallery of Ontario; Photographer: Sean Weaver; © Estate of Joyce Wieland, National Gallery of Canada (2014); Digital Image © Art Gallery of Ontario

In the 1960s, women artists reclaimed these modes of expression as a subversive means for making political statements with a highly personal—and accessible—language. Sabiston's work can be understood in the context of artists like Americans Faith Ringgold and Judy Chicago, and especially Canadian Joyce Wieland, who in works such as *The Water Quilt* (1970/71) used quilting and other needlework to explore issues of gender and nationalism. Another important consideration is the impact of the prominent women artists of the 1960s, who had established significant reputations for themselves in the mainstream art world while remaining absolutely true to their personal visions: for example, Louise Bourgeois, Alice Neel, Agnes Martin, and especially Eva Hesse, whose experimentation with material and form was of profound interest to Sabiston.

While there is most certainly a political current in Sabiston's work that connects her to these transformative figures of twentieth-century art history, her transition was also driven by a desire to engage an artistic vocabulary that would be familiar and therefore accessible to a broad audience. It was to this end that Sabiston selected textiles as a medium, and, as such, her work is also inspired by the values and vocabulary of folk art traditions. Inspirational precedents that Sabiston has noted are the quilts of Gee's Bend, a secluded African-American community located on the Alabama River. Once the site of a cotton plantation, the now renowned Gee's Bend is the locale of a nearly 200-year-old quilting tradition that originated with the slaves who worked the plantation and whose designs were more than likely inspired by the memory of patterned African textiles.

In her piecing and layering of different colours and qualities of fabric, Sabiston's technique shares certain features with the process of quilting, and her improvisational approach is comparable to the way in which Gee's Bend quilts are constructed. Her process also relates to the history of collage, a medium that has a long legacy in folk art traditions and a pivotal role in the twentieth-century avant-garde. Around 1912, Georges Braque and Pablo Picasso coined the term "collage" to describe their works that incorporated cut-and-pasted elements—such as newspaper and wallpaper—in order to challenge assumptions about what painting could be, and to infuse their work with elements of popular culture and current events. Since then, the technique has been used by many artists—including the Futurists, Dadaists, Surrealists, and Pop artists—who, like Picasso and Braque before them,

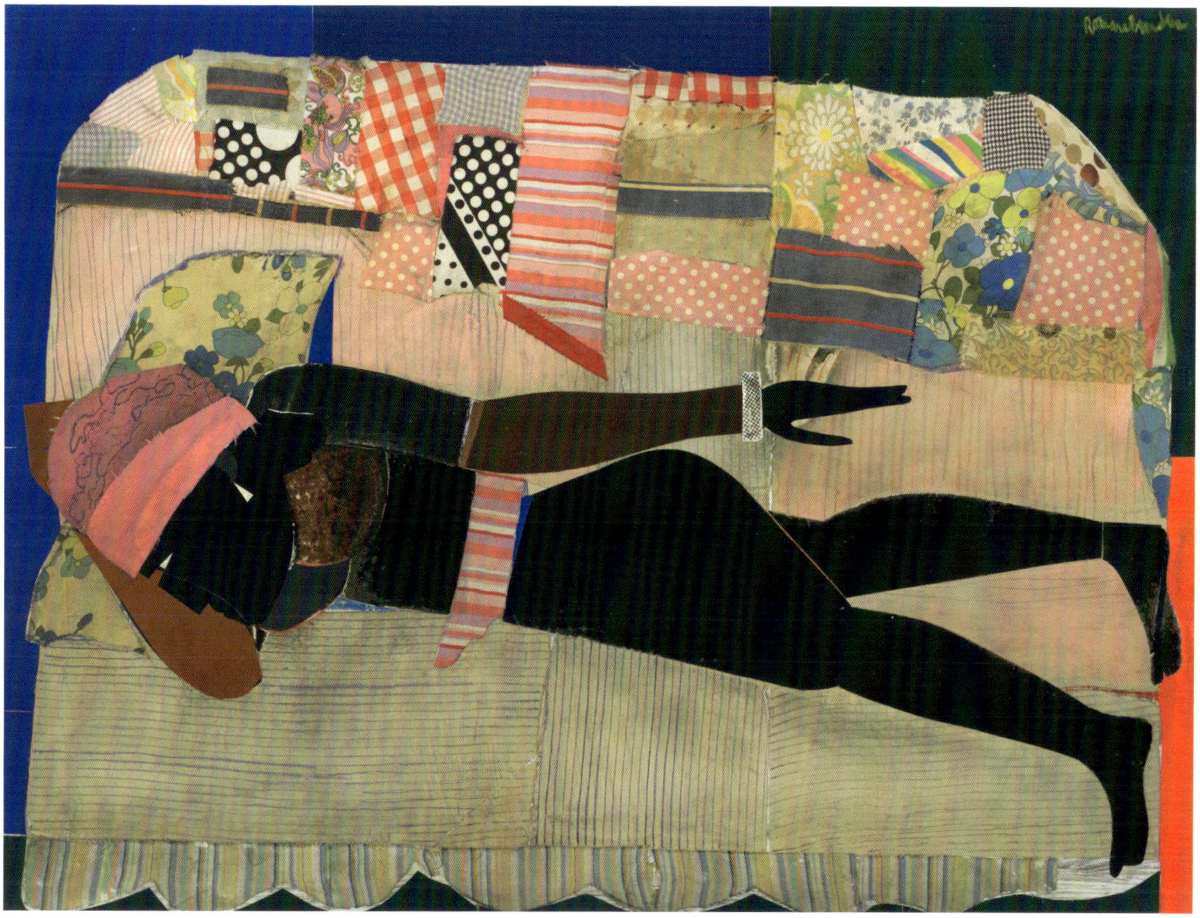

aimed to challenge the definitions and boundaries of art, life and the connections between the two.

Just prior to the moment when Sabiston developed her signature approach to textile art, certain artists were using elements of collage and assemblage in ways that would come to be recognized as transformative in the development of art production. Romare Bearden, an African-American artist associated with the Harlem Renaissance, began to use collage as a means to metaphorically deconstruct and reorder the image of Black life in civil rights-era America in works such as *Patchwork Quilt* (1970), which combines references to African-American domestic tradition with Cubism and Egyptian tomb ornament. By the 1960s, American Pop artist Robert Rauschenberg had become well known for his "combines," works variously comprising painted passages; collaged elements such as newspapers, magazines and comic books; and three-dimensional objects, including clothing, household items and even taxidermied animals.

It was Tony Urquhart, an artist based in London, Ontario, whom Sabiston met when she lived there in the mid-1960s, whose assemblages—three-dimensional boxes with painted exteriors, hinged doors and windows, and any manner of

Romare Bearden, *Patchwork Quilt*, 1970, cut-and-pasted cloth and paper with synthetic polymer paint on composition board; Collection of Museum of Modern Art; © Estate of Romare Bearden, VAGA, New York / SODRAC, Montreal (2014); Digital Image ©The Museum of Modern Art/ Licensed by SCALA/Art Resource, NY

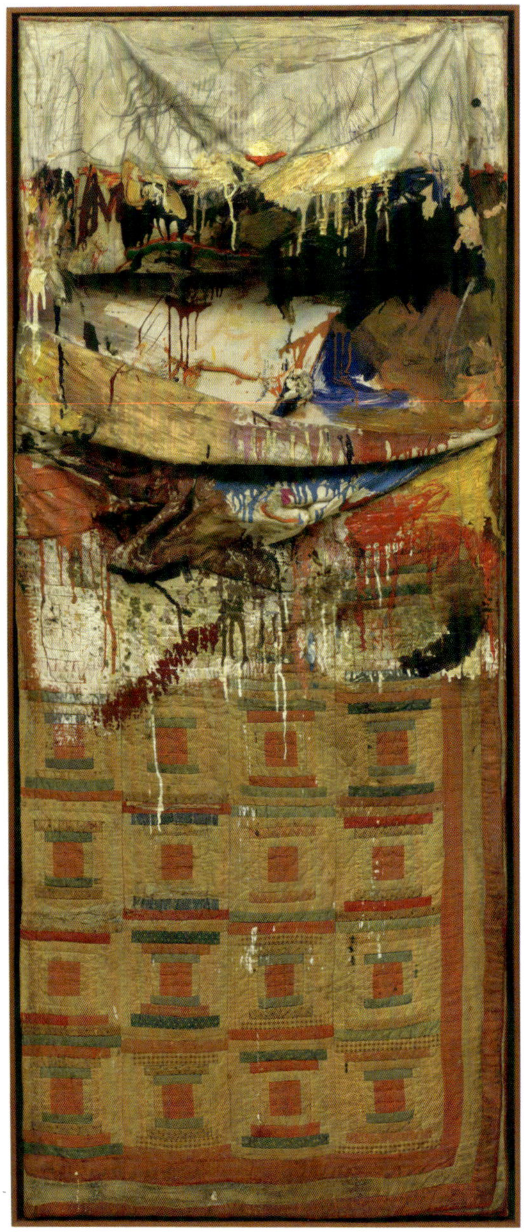

Robert Rauschenberg, *Bed*, 1955, oil and pencil on pillow, quilt and sheet on wood supports; Collection of Museum of Modern Art; © Estate of Robert Rauschenberg, SODRAC, Montreal/ VAGA, New York (2014); Digital Image ©The Museum of Modern Art/Licensed by SCALA / Art Resource, NY

affixed found objects—were of direct interest to her. She acknowledges him as an inspiration for "his use of everything."[1] Sabiston's approach to collage, though, is also linked to the medium's often-overlooked long history. In a 1974 text, Melissa Meyer and Miriam Schapiro, two pioneers of feminist art, brought attention to the fact that collage was "a word invented in the twentieth century to describe an activity with an ancient history."[2] Schapiro and Meyer, in turn, invented the word "femmage" to describe the disregarded history of collage as it had been "practiced by women using traditional women's techniques to achieve their art—sewing, piecing, hooking, cutting, appliquéing, cooking and the like—activities also engaged in by men but assigned to the history of women."[3] As Schapiro and Meyer wrote,

> *We feel that several criteria determine whether a work can be called femmage. Not all of them appear in a single object. However, the presence of at least half of them should allow the work to be appreciated as femmage.*
>
> ***1. It is a work by a woman. 2. The activities of saving and collecting are important ingredients. 3. Scraps are essential to the process and are recycled in the work. 4. The theme has a woman-life context. 5. The work has elements of covert imagery. 6. The theme of the work addresses itself to an audience of intimates. 7. It celebrates a private or public event. 8. A diarist's point of view is reflected in the work. 9. There is drawing and/or handwriting sewn in the work. 10. It contains silhouetted images which are fixed on material. 11. Recognizable images appear in narrative sequence. 12. Abstract forms create a pattern. 13. The work contains photographs or other printed matter. 14. The work has a functional as well as an aesthetic life.***[4]

Sabiston's work certainly fulfills the requirements of femmage. But alongside this contextualization within the histories of folk art, feminist art and collage, her work has also remained connected to the formal concerns that occupied her as a painter. She uses larger fields of colour layered with detail to create compositions that often depict the elemental components of earth, sea and sky and thus lean towards the history of landscape painting, although concerns of abstract image-making are also manifest in Sabiston's work, and questions regarding the relationship of form and colour, surface and spatial illusion are also important considerations for her. Just as she merges craft and fine art, so too she brings together issues related to both representation and abstraction. While Sabiston's work certainly shows evidence of painterly precedents, they tend to be eclectic and can manifest as a philosophical influence rather than a formal one. From the recurring presence of the diagonal in her compositions (for which precedents can be found in the work of artists as various as Tintoretto, Peter Paul Rubens, and Edgar Degas), to the inclination to create, like Emily Carr, Jack Shadbolt and Gordon Smith—all icons of BC art—compositions that are infused with her personal experience of the West Coast environment, it is evident that despite her new pursuits, Sabiston never fully turned her back on painting.

Although there are inevitable ties to each of these histories, the challenge of situating Sabiston within narratives of folk, decorative or feminist art, collage or painting is that these contextualizations ignore the multidisciplinary nature of her production. Her earliest architectural commissions were tapestries produced for the Skyline Hotel chain in 1971—fabric collages that were influenced by her previous experience designing costumes for theatre. She has described how her time in the theatre inspired her to be collaborative and to think about how her work related to the qualities of its setting and even to the people that would occupy and move in the space.[5] This mode of creating works that are functional, site-specific, kinetic, collaborative and cross-disciplinary situates Sabiston in a lineage of artists, including Sonia Delaunay, Alexander Calder, Friedensreich Hundertwasser, and Canadian Aiko Suzuki, who also deftly brought disciplines together in their work.

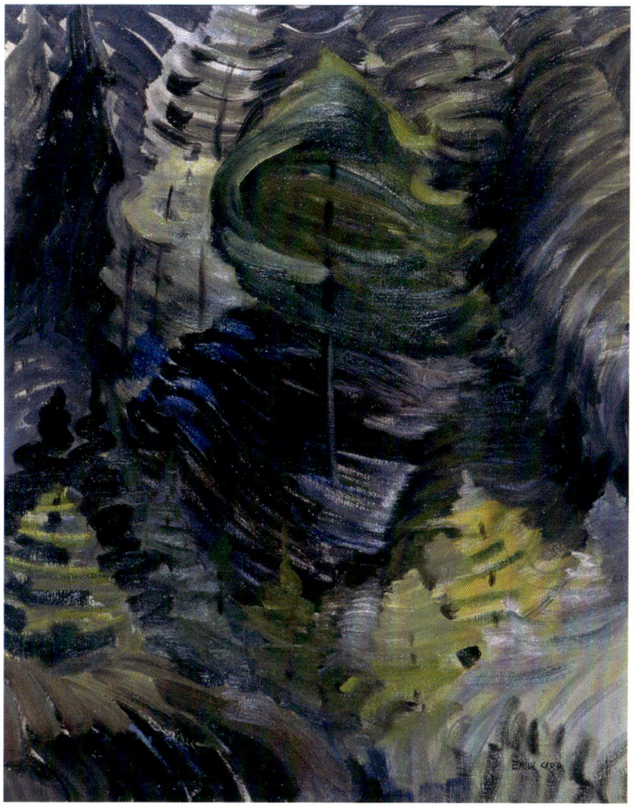

Emily Carr, *Juice of Life*, 1939, oil on canvas; Collection of Art Gallery of Greater Victoria; Photographer: Stephen Topfer

At the outset of her career as a textile artist, Sabiston faced dismissal, or even derision, from

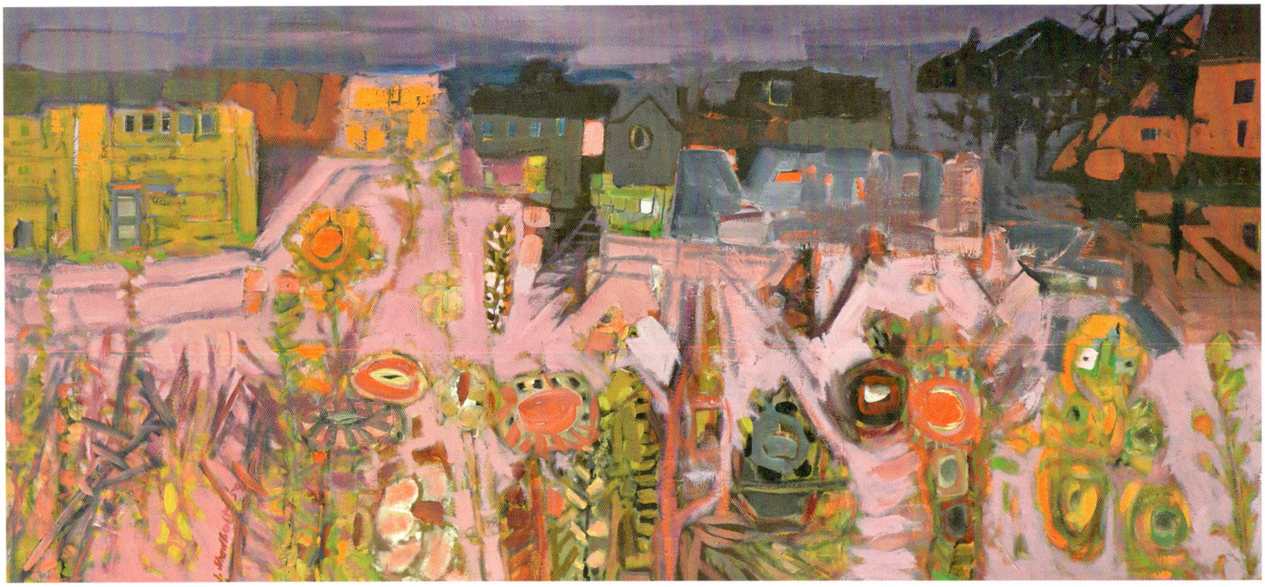

Jack Shadbolt, *Abandoned Mining Town*, 1959, oil on canvas; Collection of Art Gallery of Greater Victoria; Photographer: Stephen Topfer; © Estate of Jack Shadbolt, Simon Fraser University Art Galleries (2014)

some members of Canada's art establishment because of her choice of medium. Without doubt, she was part of the movement that brought the vocabularies of craft and women's work into the realm of contemporary art. Today she can be considered a forerunner in an expanding community of Canadian artists who unapologetically use methods of craft to produce contemporary art: Dorothy Caldwell, Kai Chan, David R. Harper, Luanne Martineau, Lyn Carter, Heather Goodchild and Allyson Mitchell are just a few. At the same time, although Sabiston uses feminist materials and strategies, much of her work has been produced as an integral element in the context of architecture or public space, arenas which have historically been deemed masculine. It was invited, commissioned and presumably welcomed to function in these realms. As a result, we have perhaps tended to overlook her feminist and political content and strategies. Ultimately, Sabiston holds a singular place in the art world, defined by a myriad of influences and legacies. While an attempt has been made here to trace a narrative that situates her œuvre, in actuality, pinning her work into art history will always be something of an improvisational pursuit, an exercise in connecting threads.

Endnotes

1. Carole Sabiston, personal communication with Michelle Jacques, August 8, 2013.
2. Miriam Schapiro and Melissa Meyer, "Waste Not Want Not: An Inquiry into What Women Saved and Assembled – FEMMAGE," in *Theories and Documents of Contemporary Art: A Sourcebook of Artists' Writings*, ed. Kristine Stiles and Peter Selz (Berkeley: University of California Press, 1996), 151.
3. Ibid., 152
4. Ibid., 153.
5. Sandra Alfoldy, *The Allied Arts: Architecture and Crafts in Postwar Canada* (Montreal and Kingston: McGill-Queen's University Press, 2012), 80.

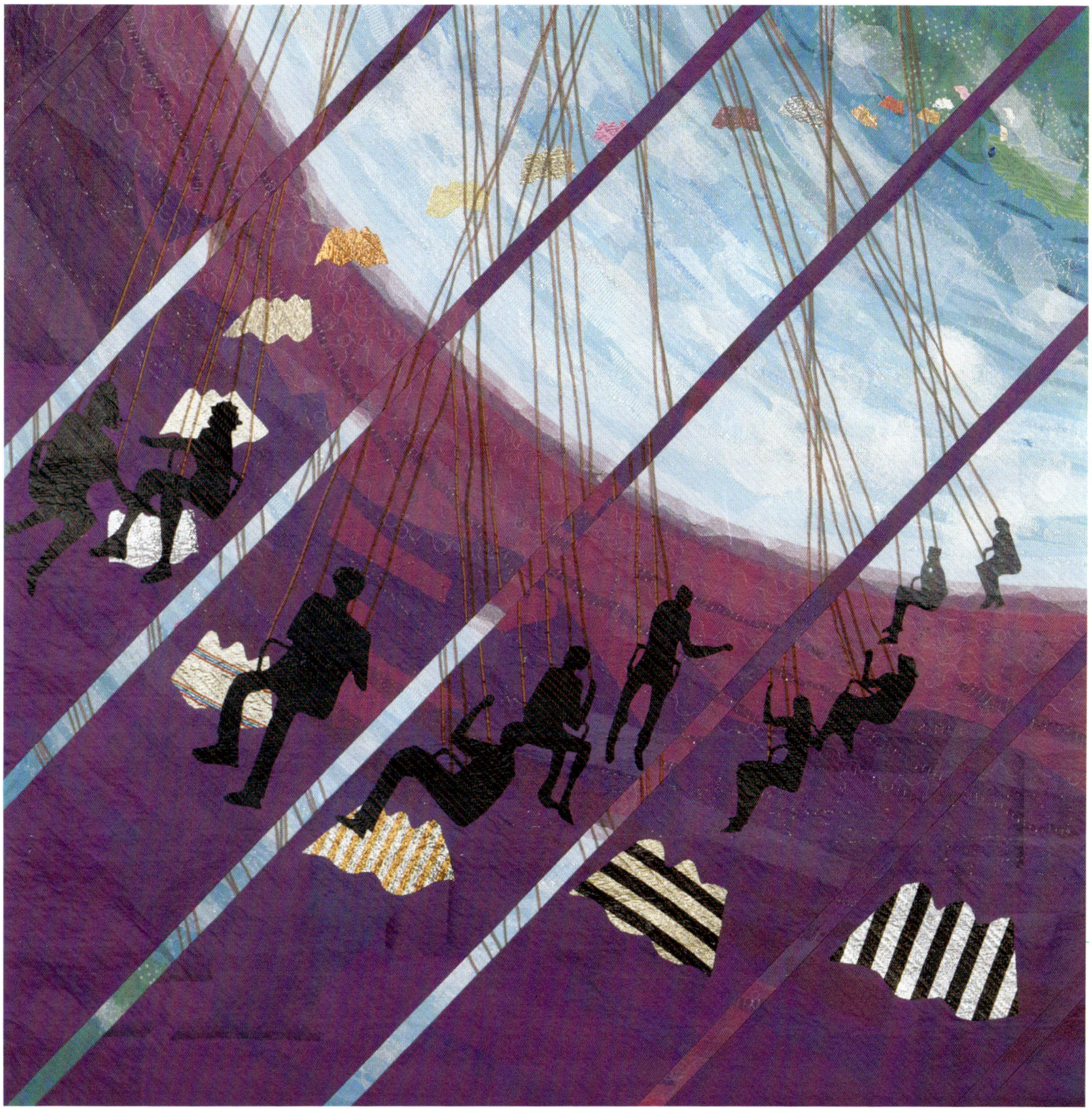

cat. 18 *Spatial Possibilities: Individual Take Off*, 1988

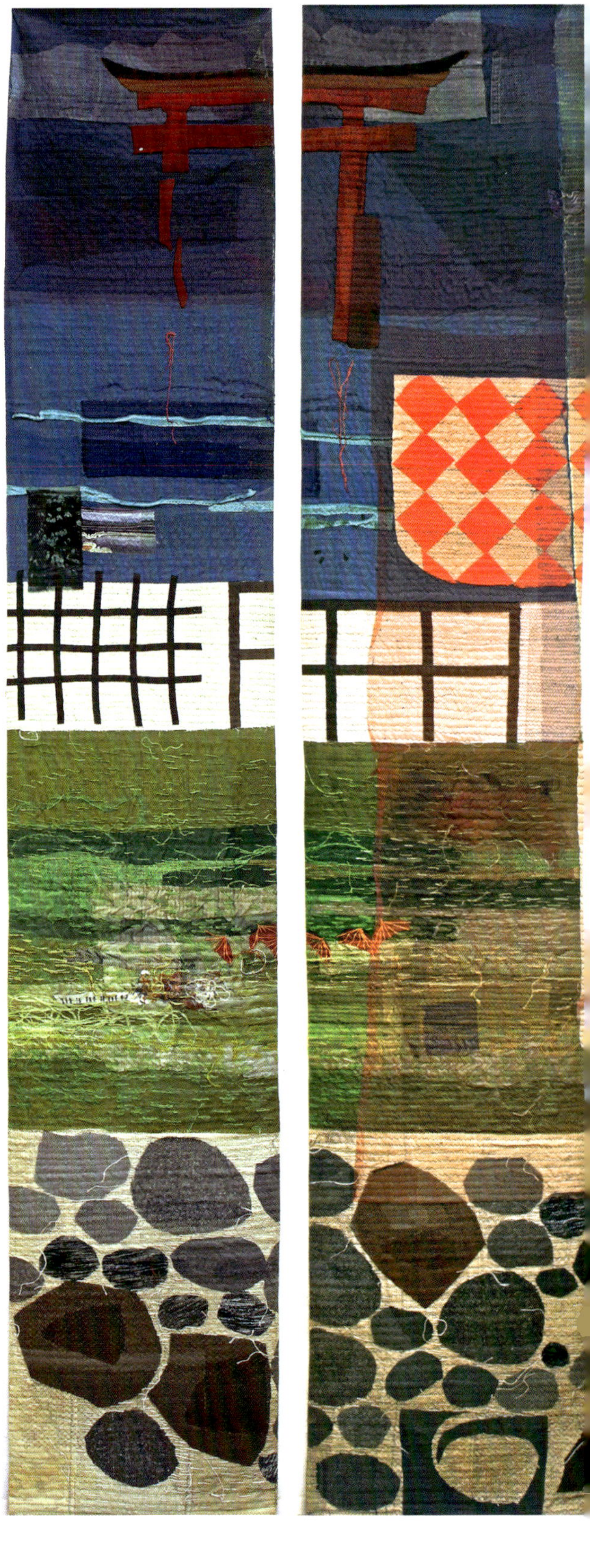

cat. 4 *Japan Journey*, 1979

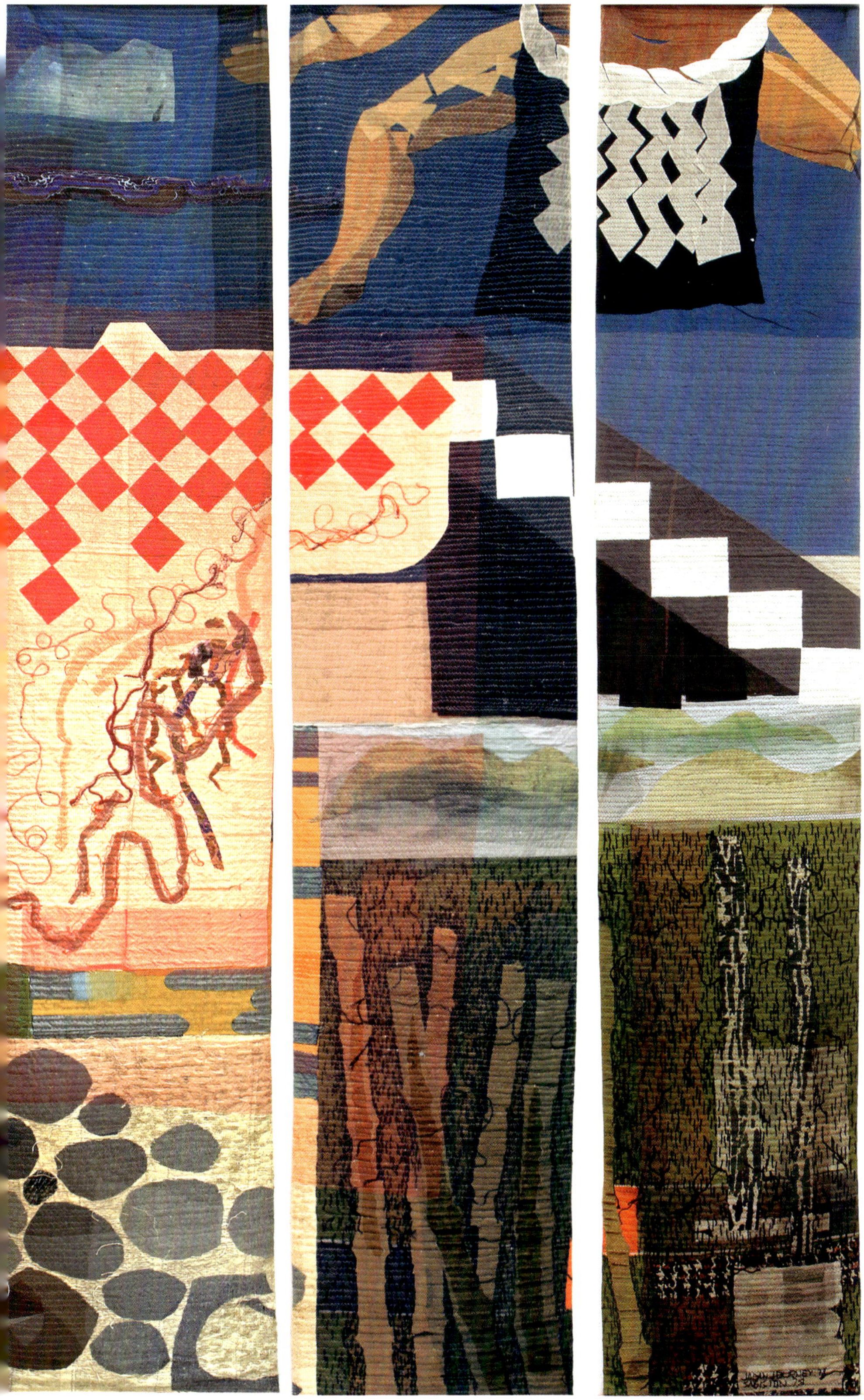

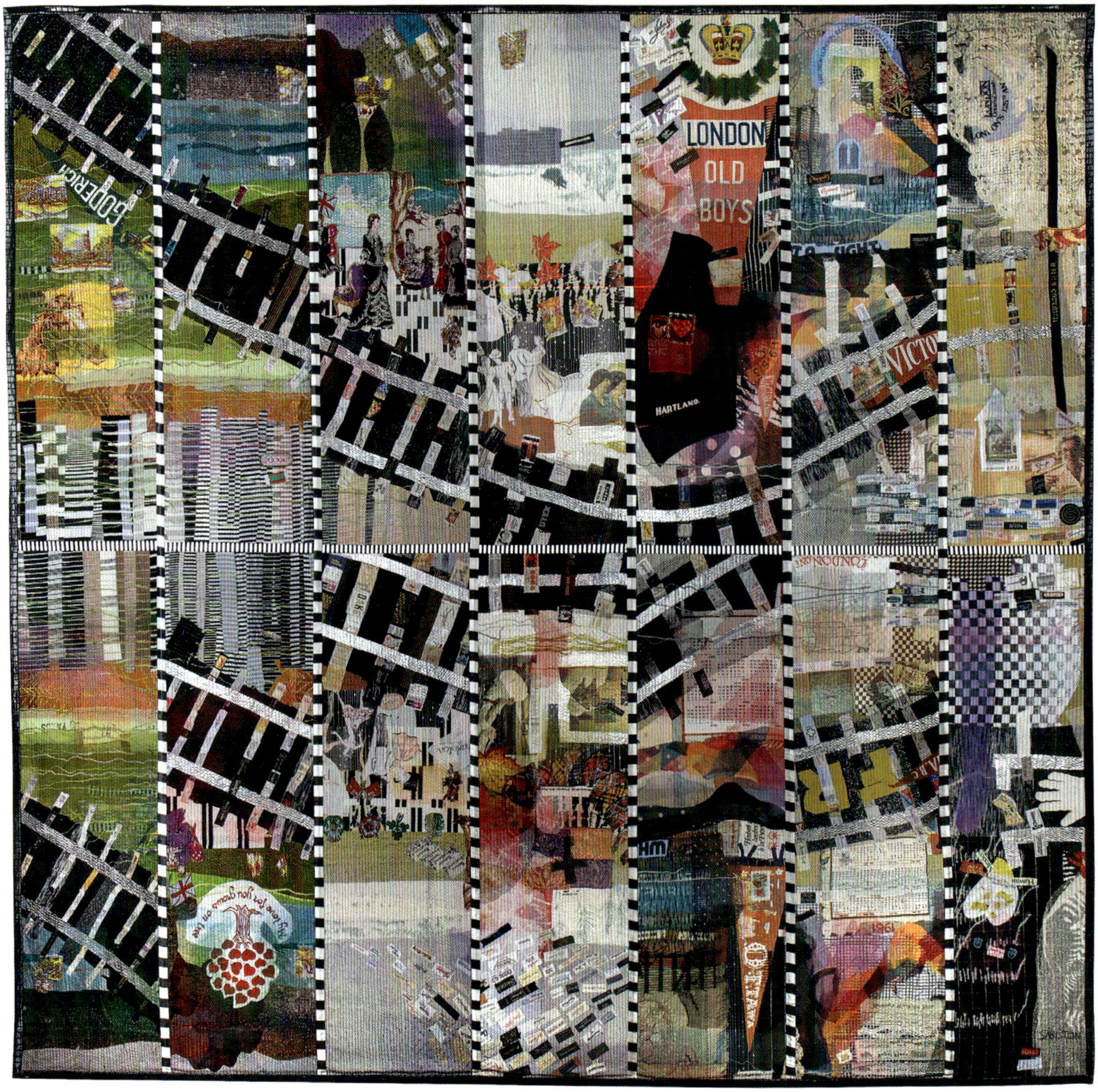

cat. 6 *Moving Through a Fragmented London Life*, 1981

cat. 23 *Points of Ocean View*, 1992

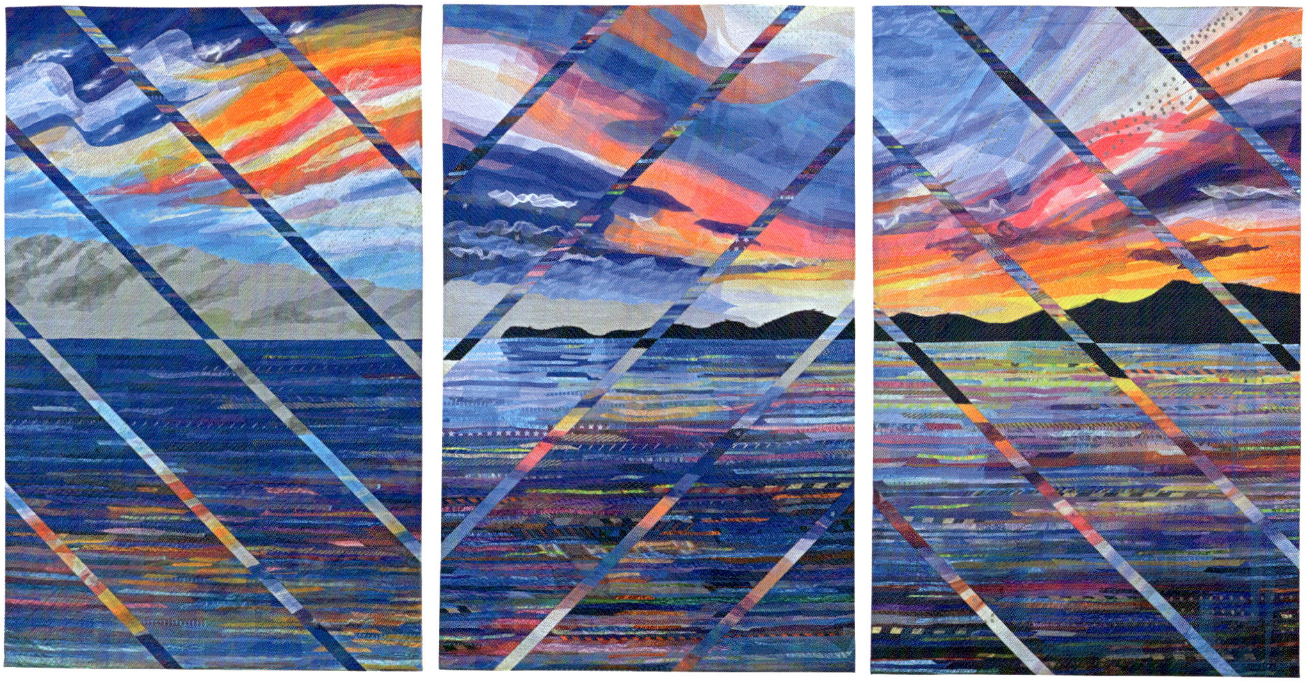

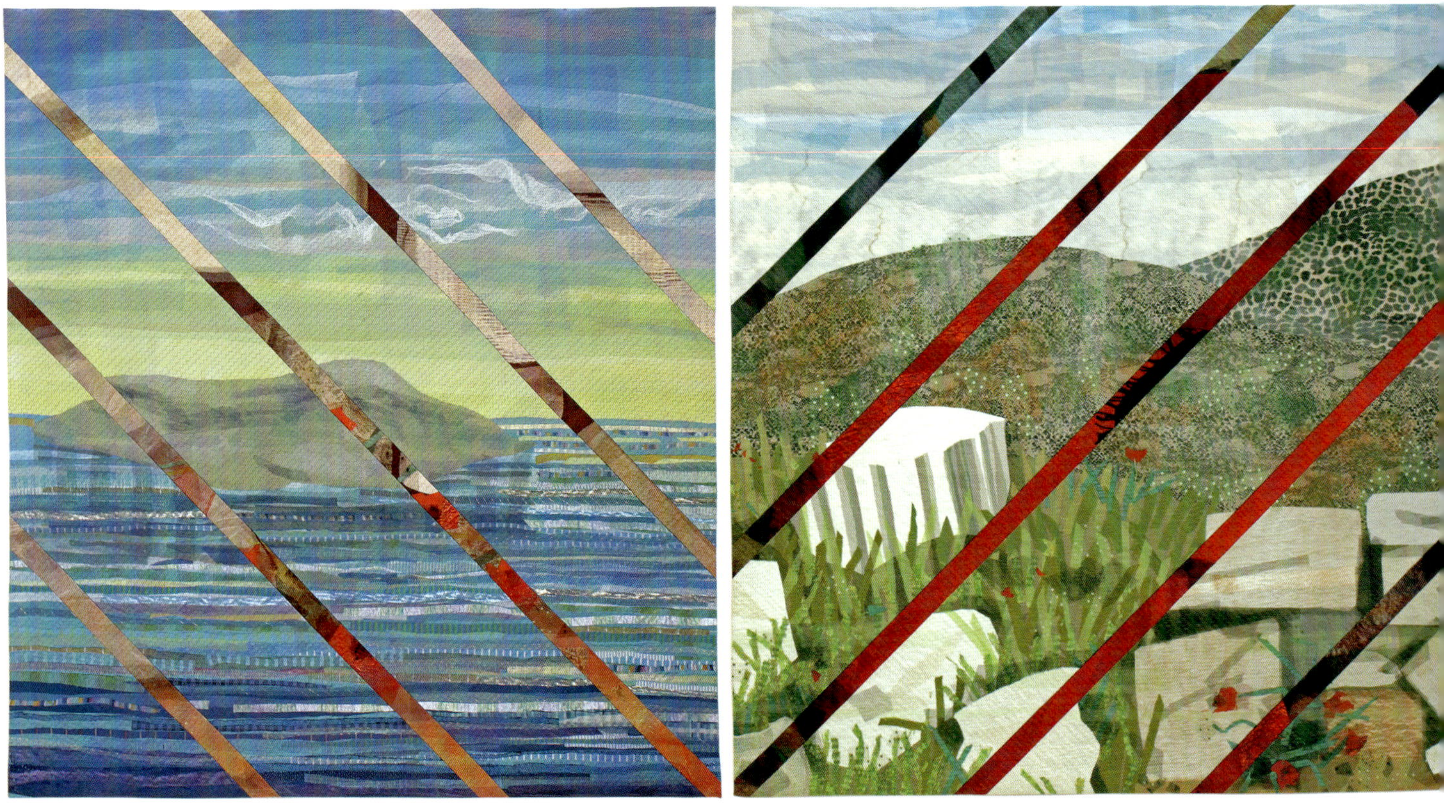

cat. 21 *Flying into Delos*, 1992

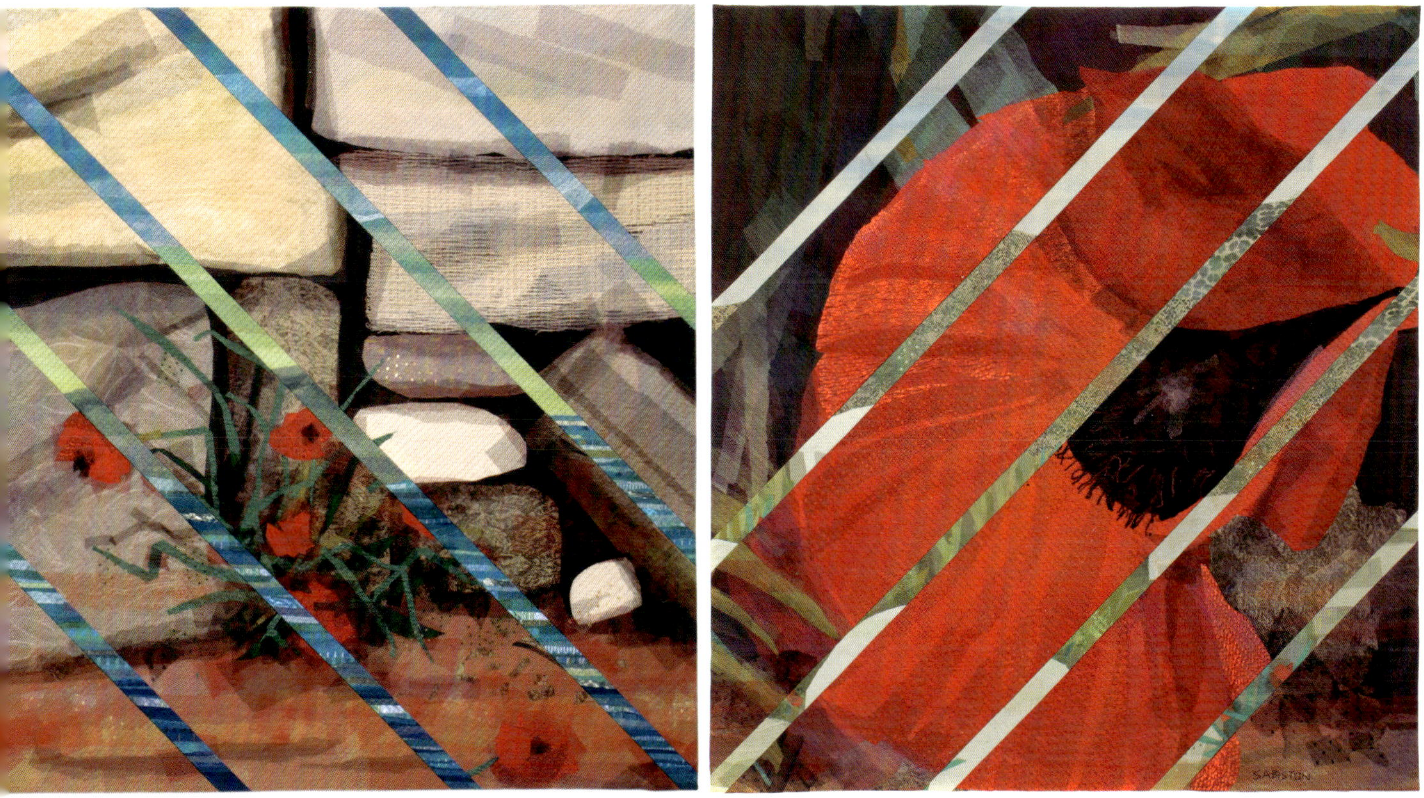
SABISTON

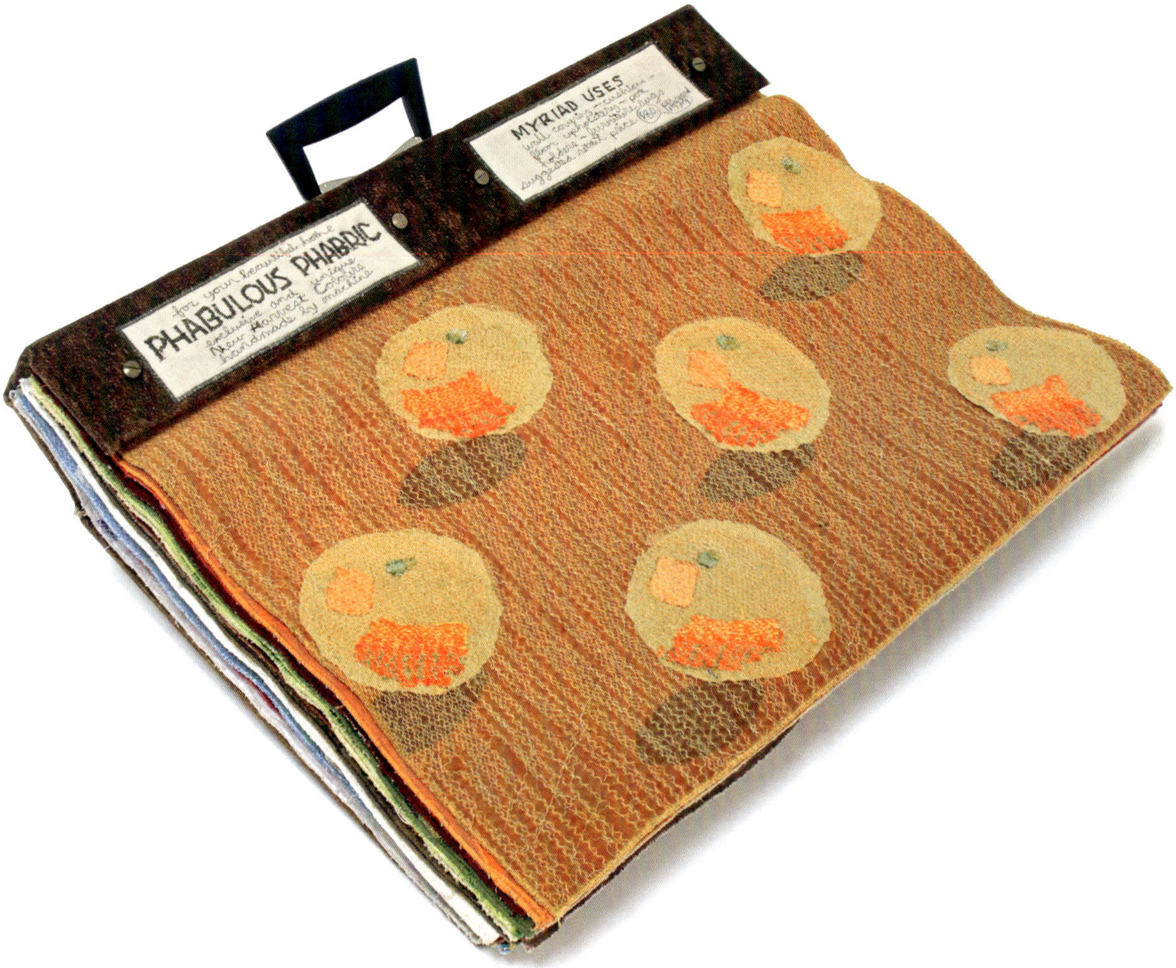

cat. 5 *Phabulous Phabrics*; (details) *Banana*, *Baby Blue*, *Salmon*, 1979

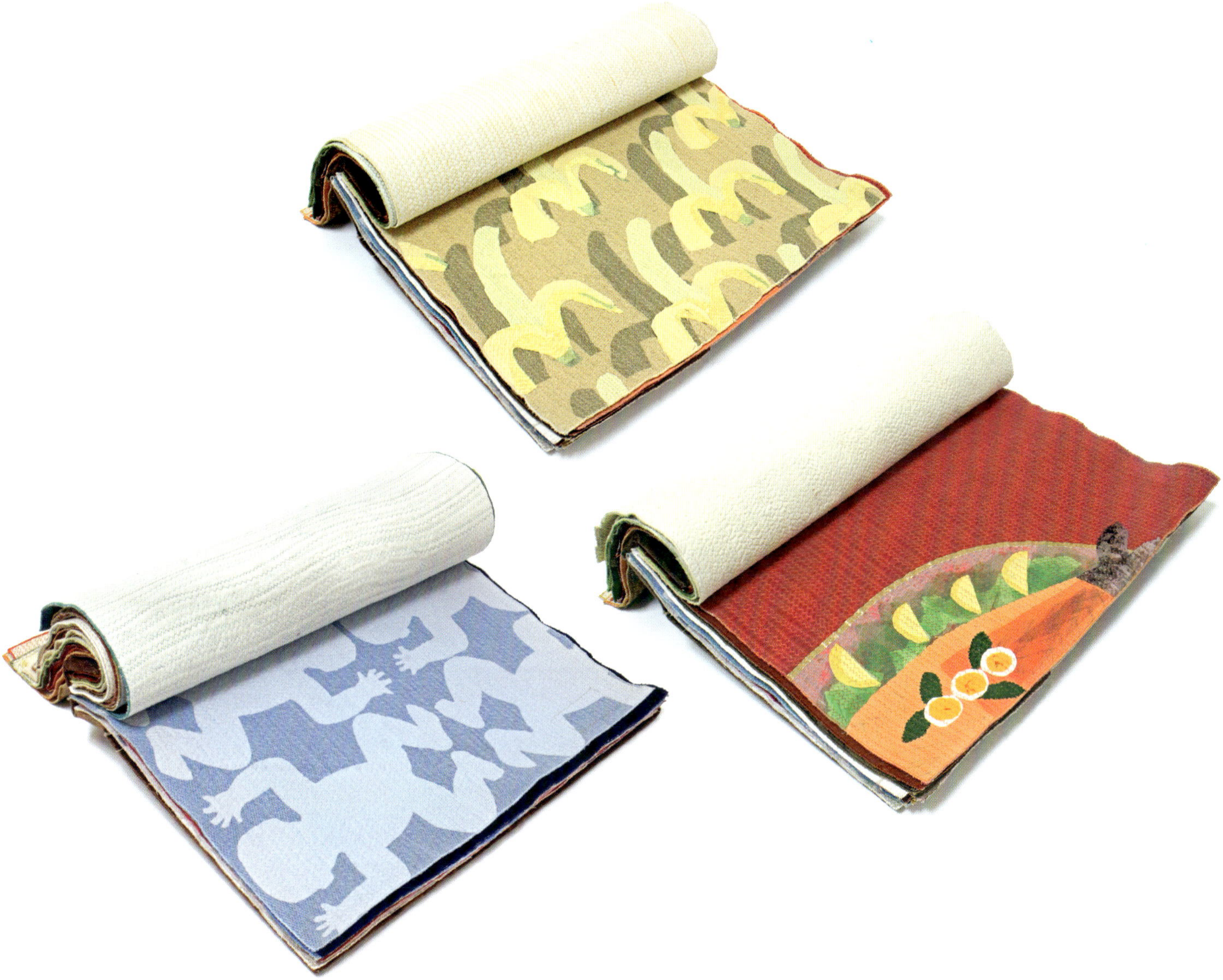

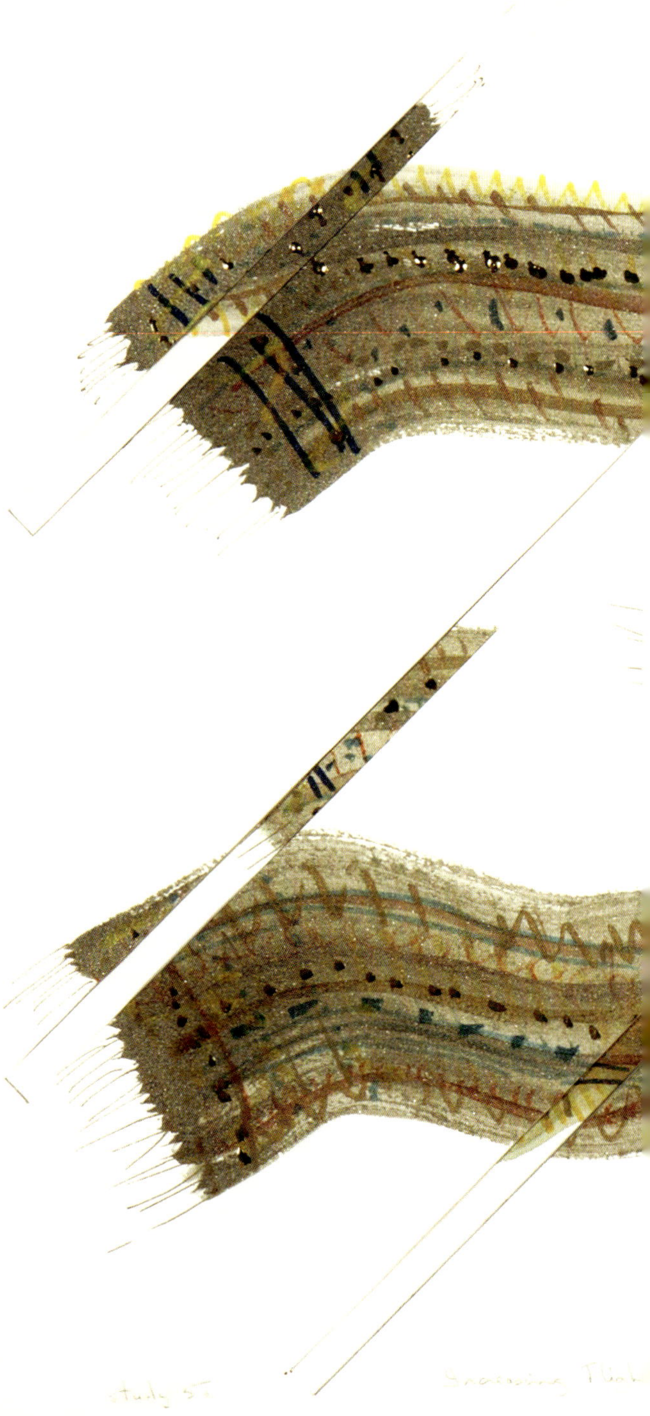

cat. 40 *Flying Carpets Study #5*, 1990

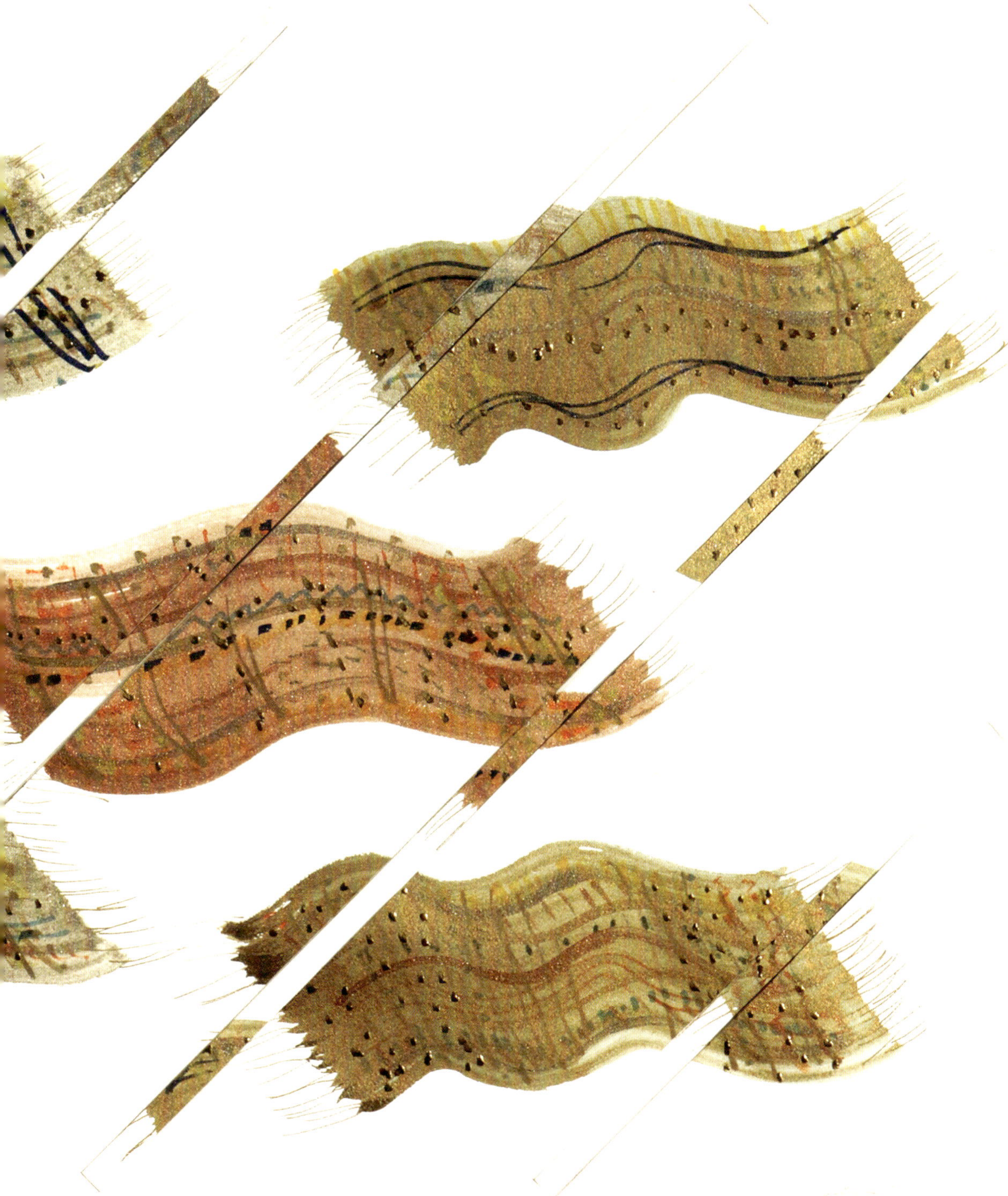

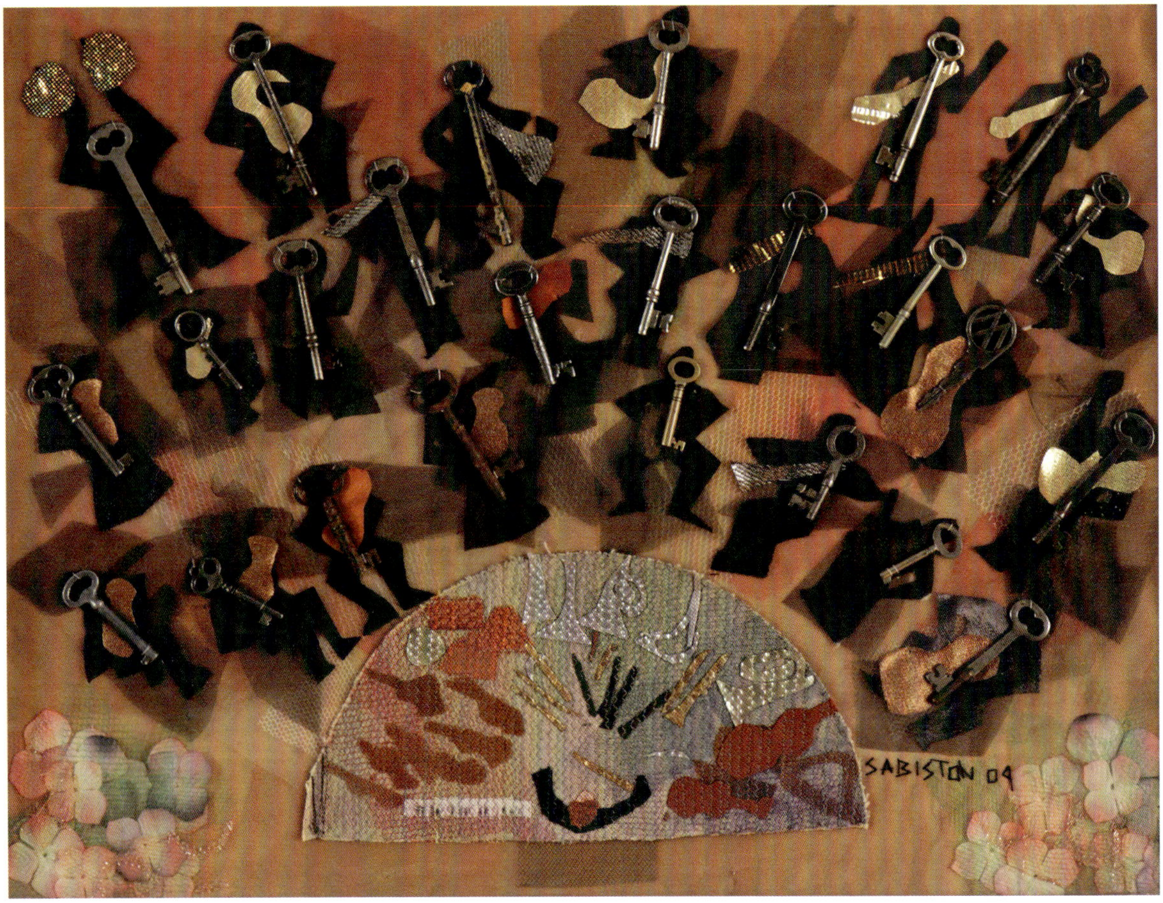

cat. 29 *Opus #1: In the Key of ?*, 2009

cat. 24 *Flying Revolution Quartet* (lower right quadrant), 1993

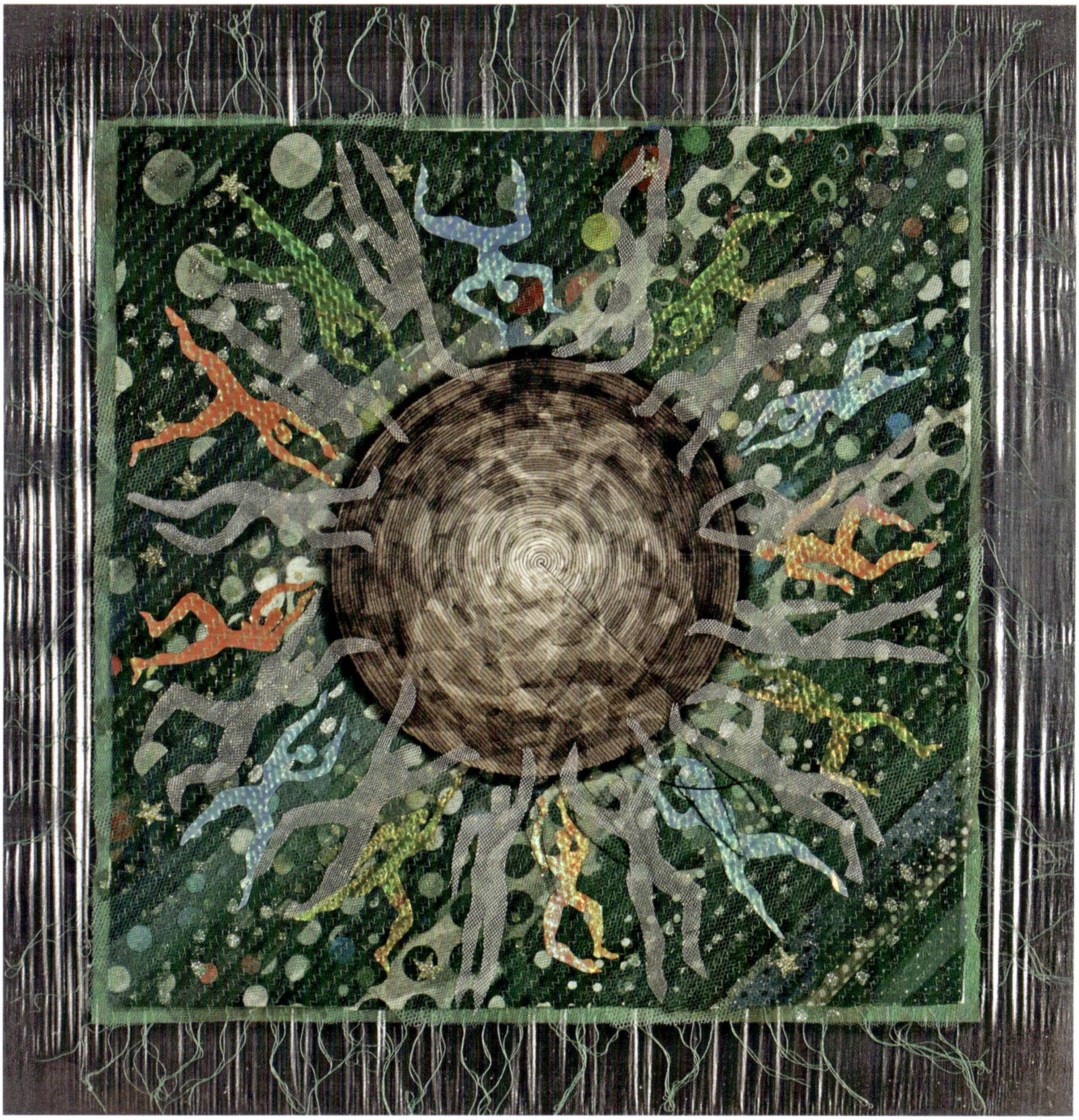

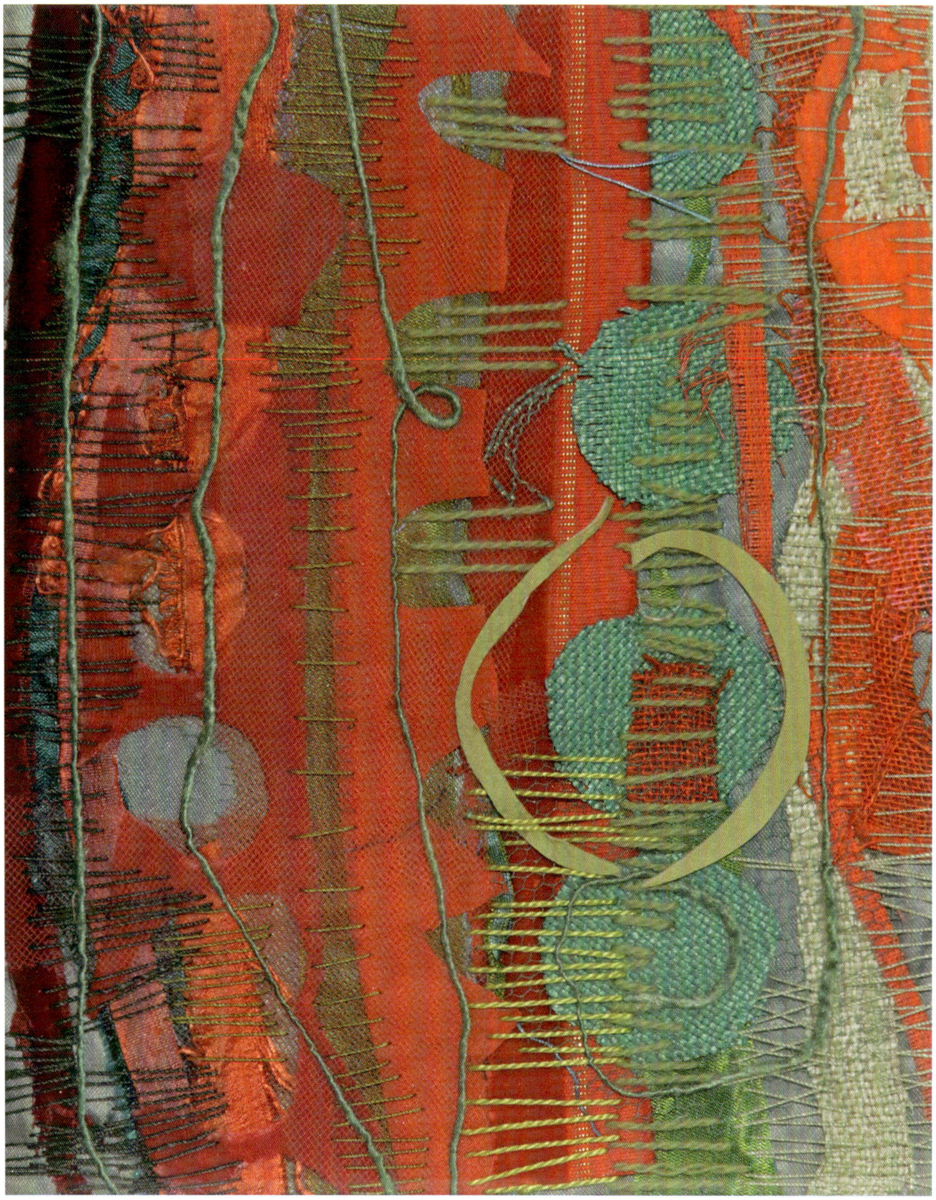

cat. 3 *Colour Study: Red Garden*, 1976

cat. 2 *Colour Study: Blue Rain*, 1976

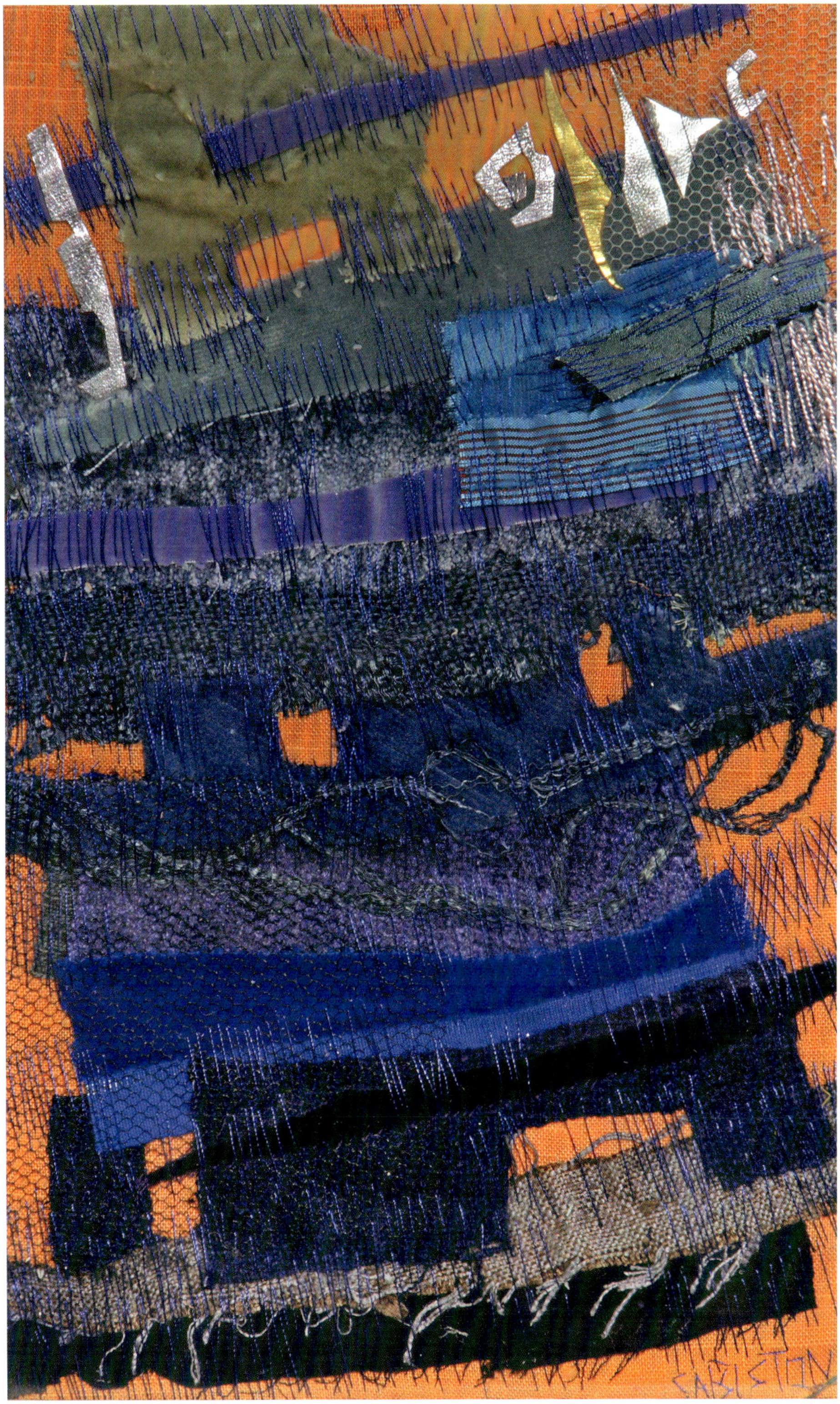

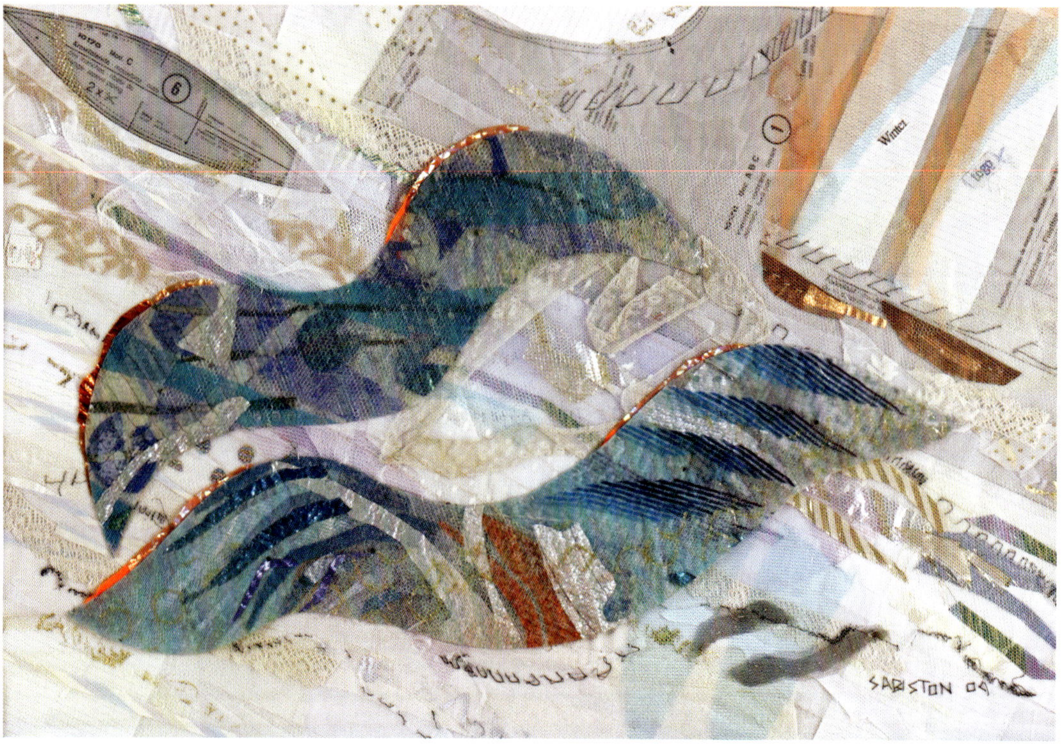

cat. 27 *Flight Patterns*, 2009

cat. 28 *Fly the Horizon*, 2009

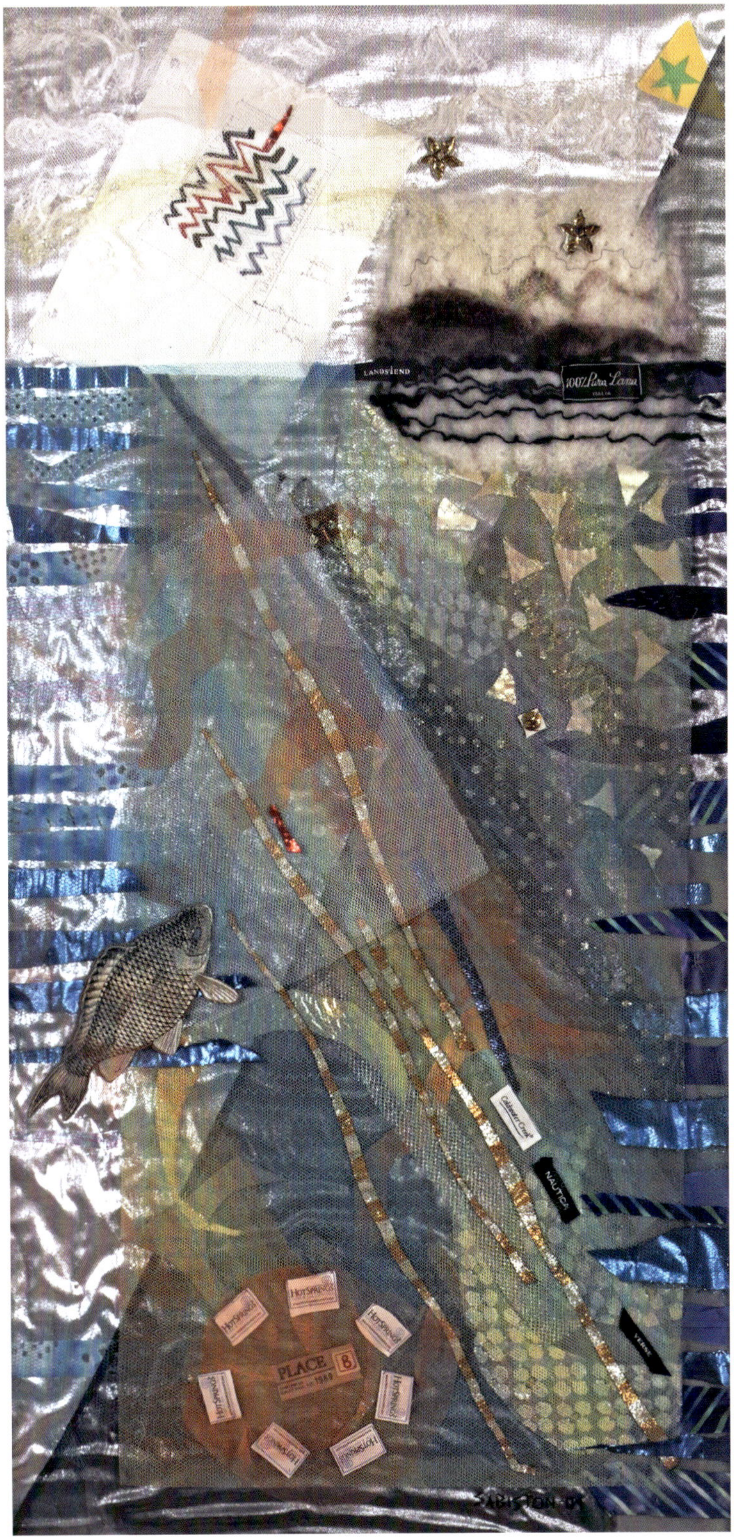

LANDS' END
100% Pura Lana
NAUTICA
PLACE 8

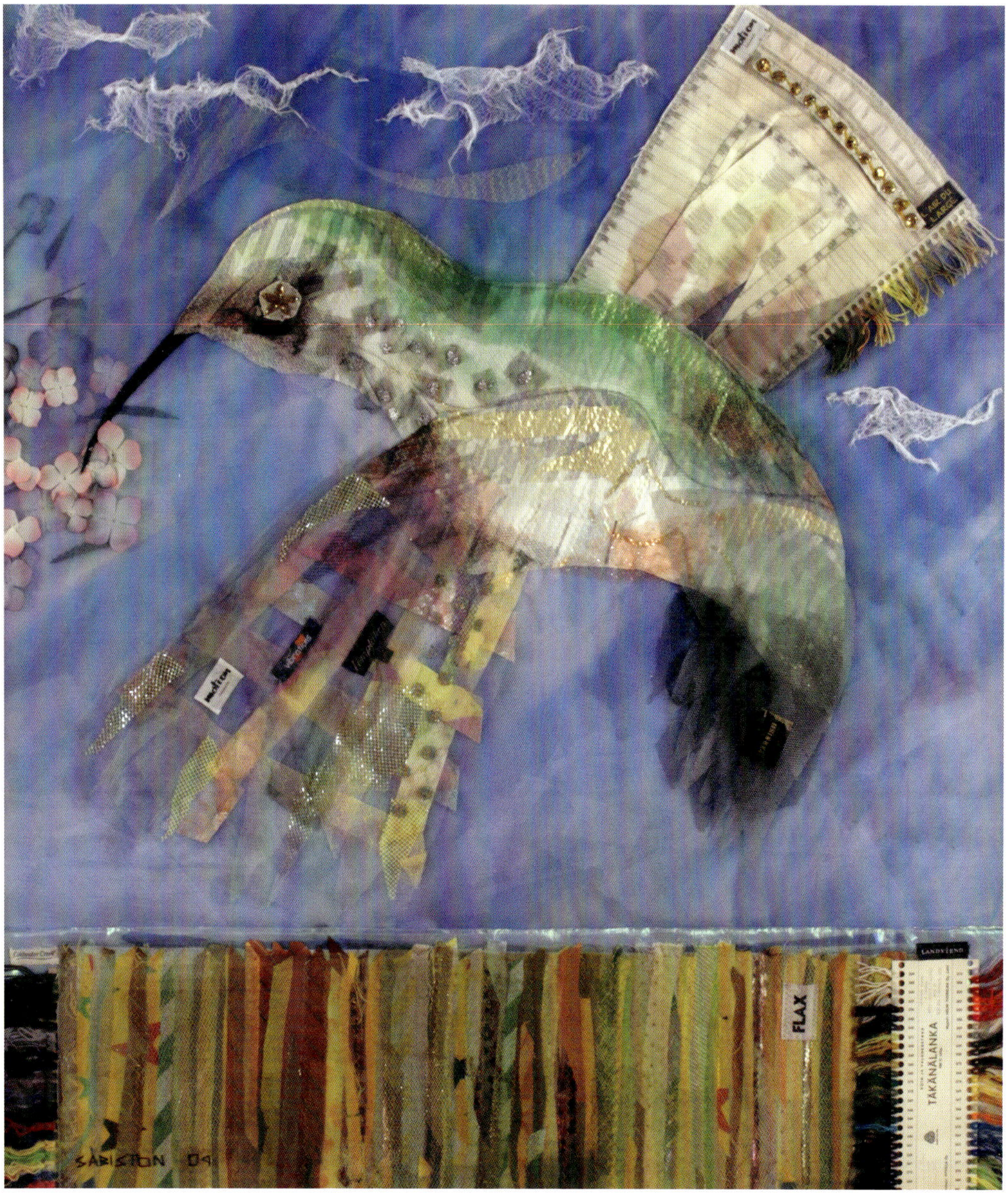

cat. 26 *Flying Rufus*, 2009

cat. 32 *Pockets for Men's Trousers*, 2013 (background panel in progress)

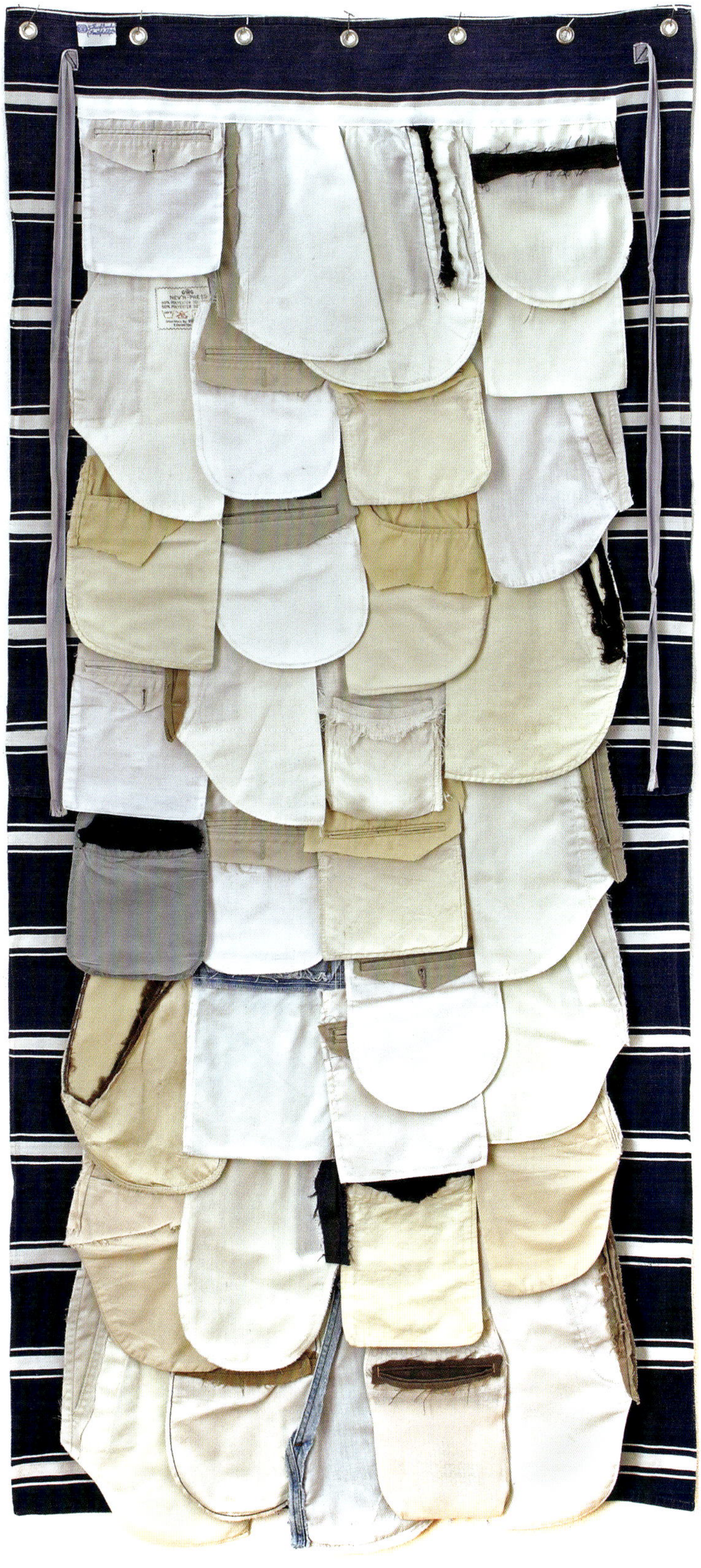

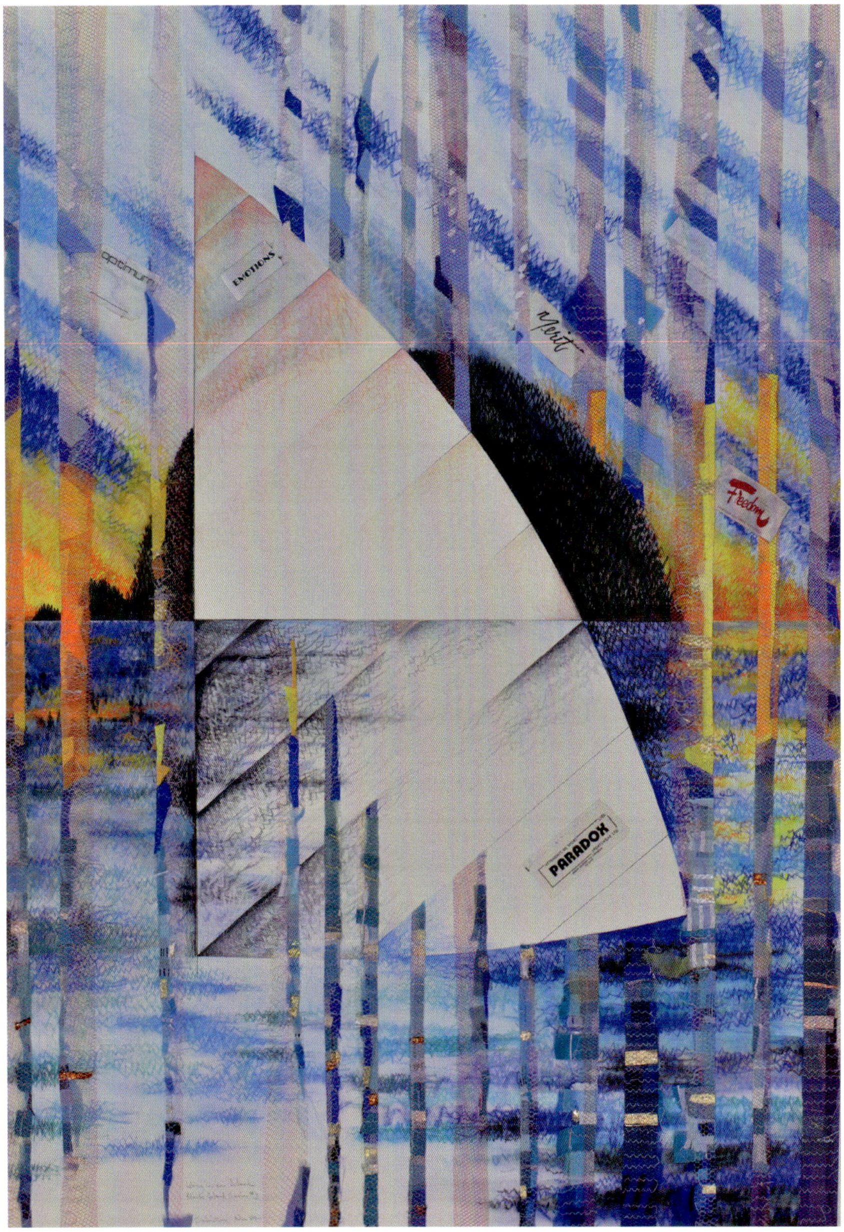

cat. 9 *Living in an Island*, 1984

cat. 20 *Two Bits of Sky: Day and Night*, 1990/91

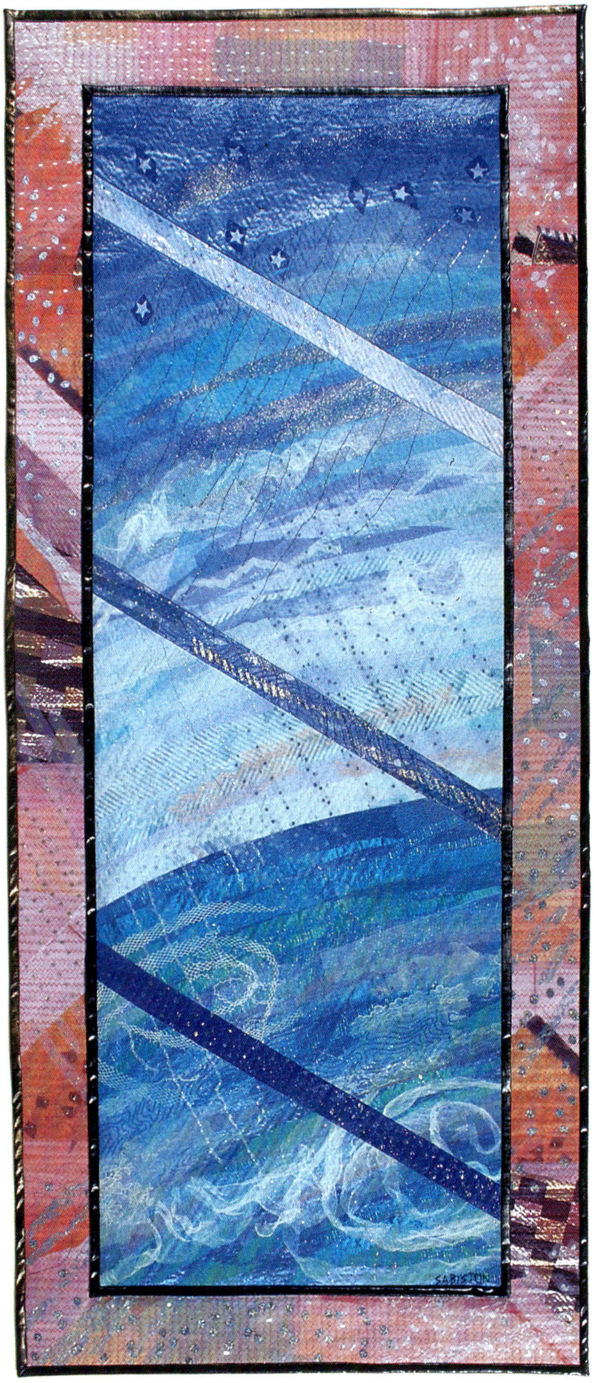
SABISTON

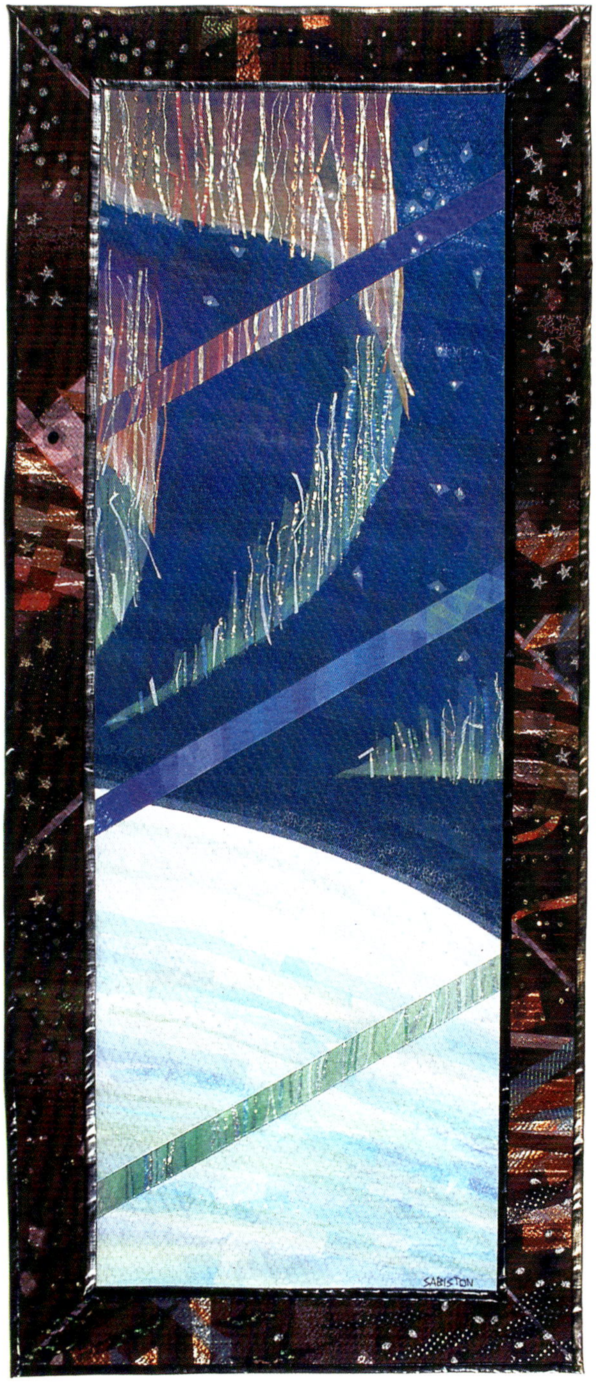
SABISTON

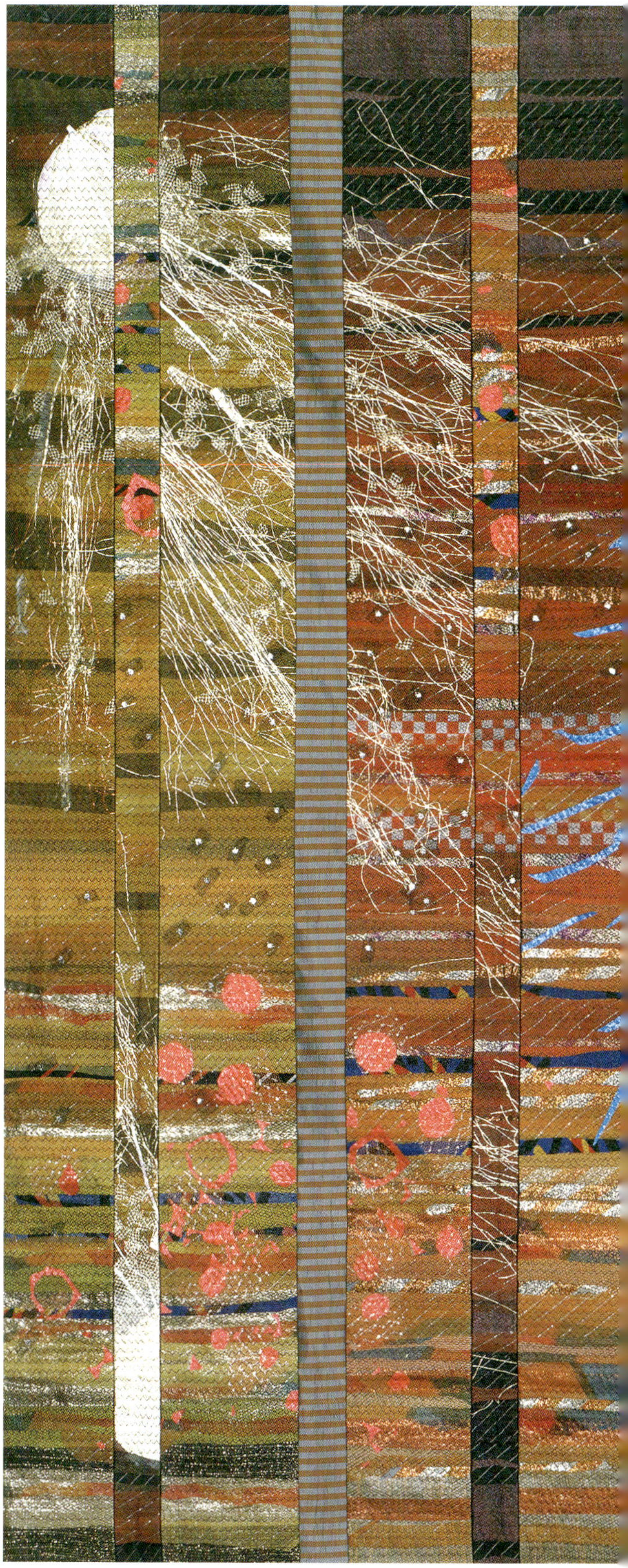

cat. 10 *Royal Fireworks Suite*, 1984

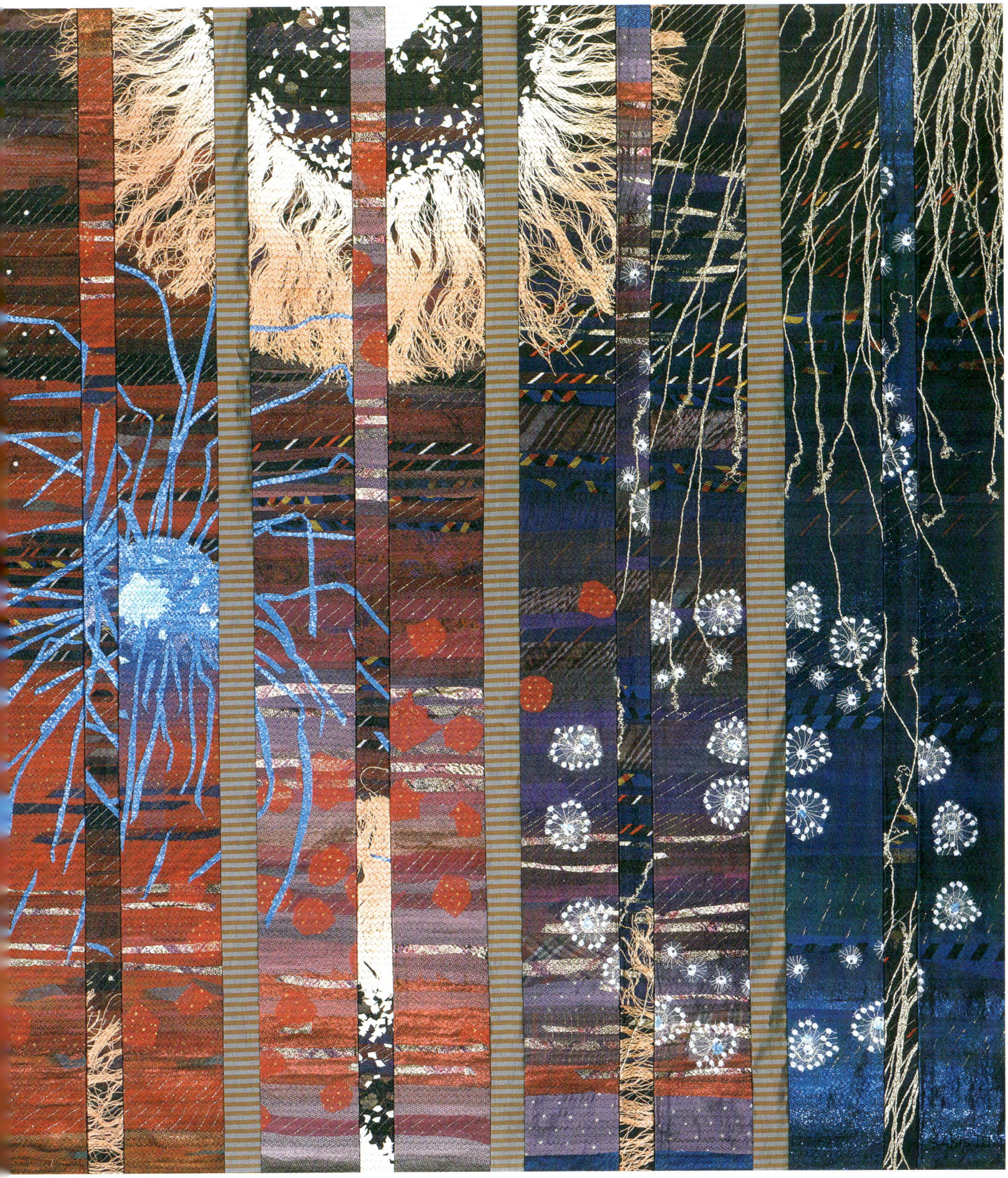

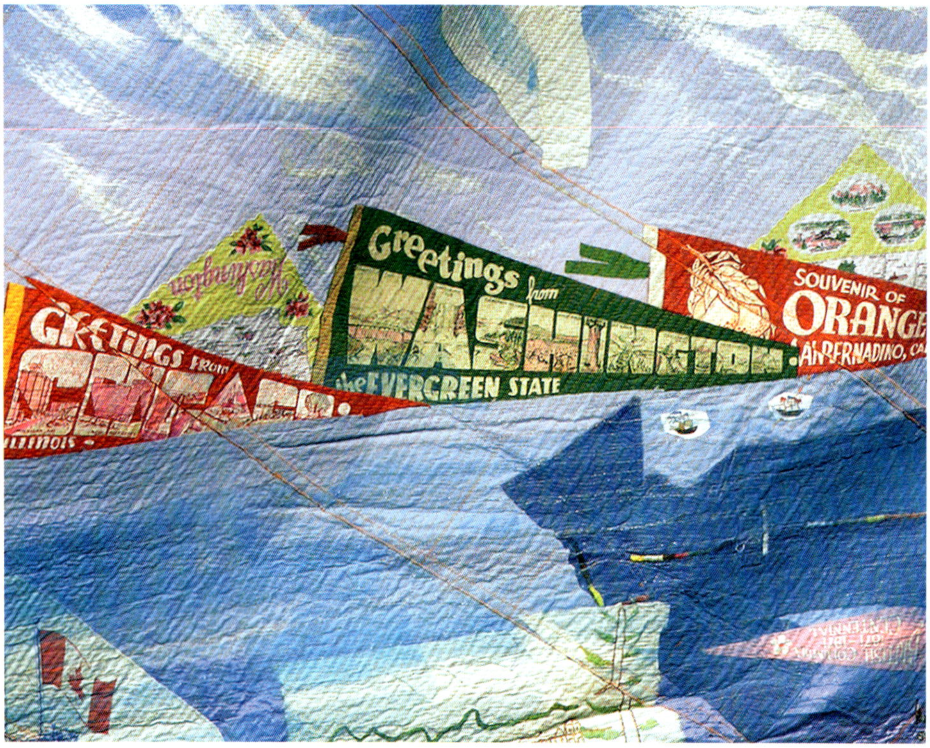

cat. 8 *Sailing: Victorian Secondhand Sail; New-raw-tick Dawn* (detail), 1982

cat. 8 *Sailing: Victorian Secondhand Sail; New-raw-tick Dawn*, 1982, and cat. 7 *Sailing: Dotti O'verdose; All That Glitters*, 1982

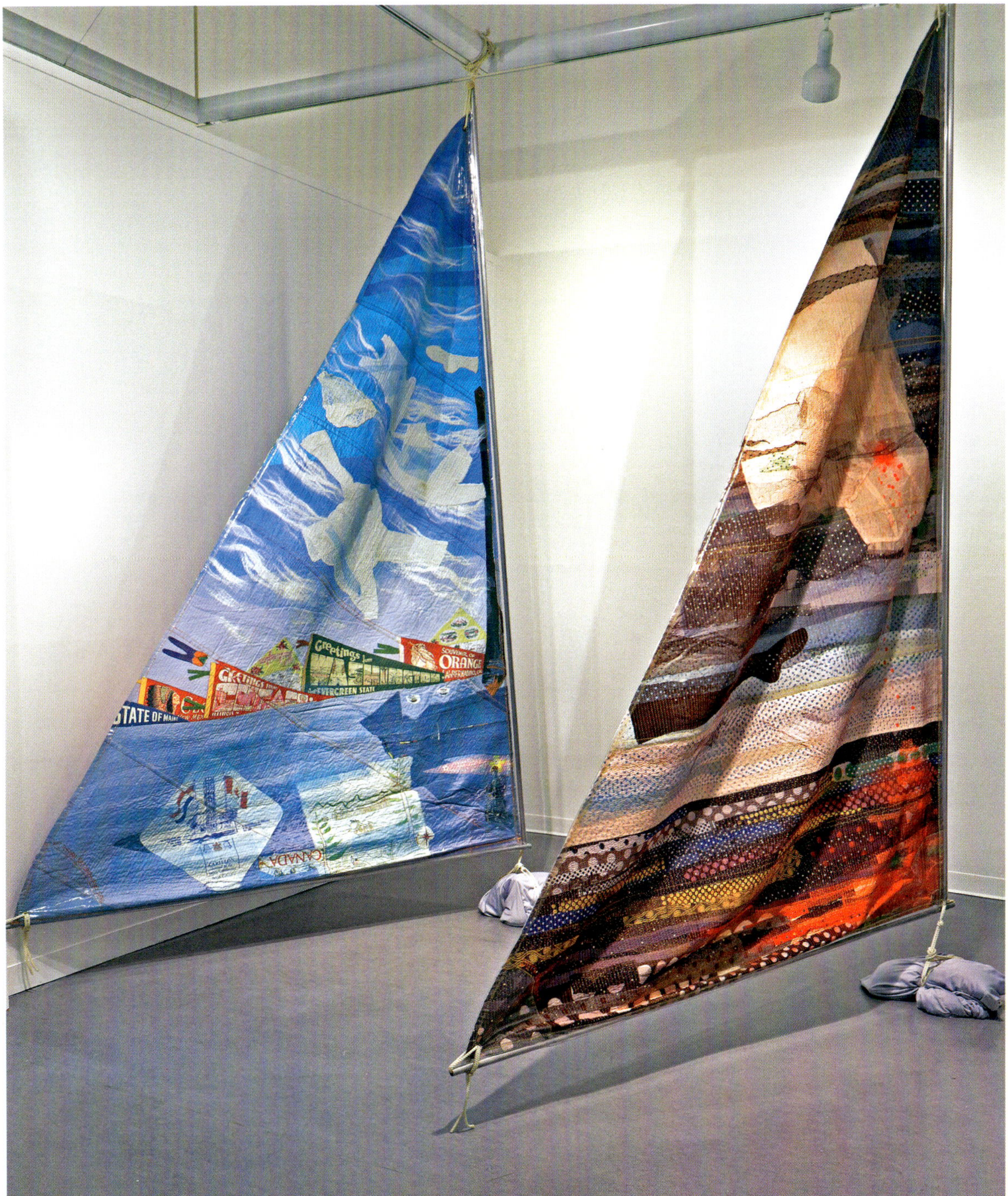

Greetings
SOUVENIR OF
ORANGE
EVERGREEN STATE
CANADA

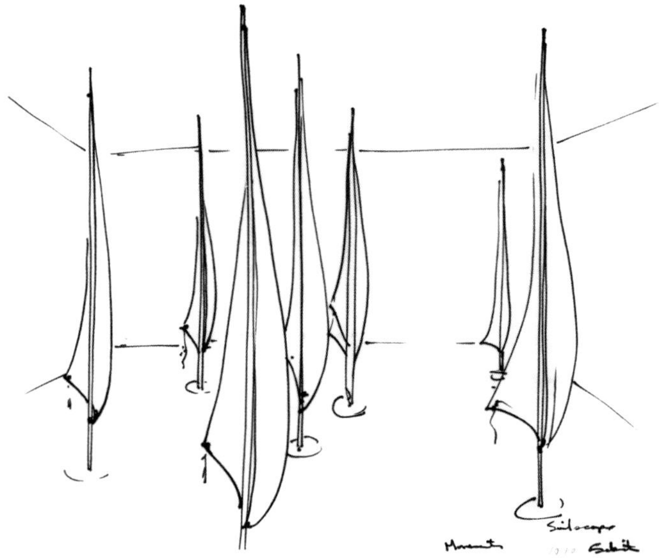

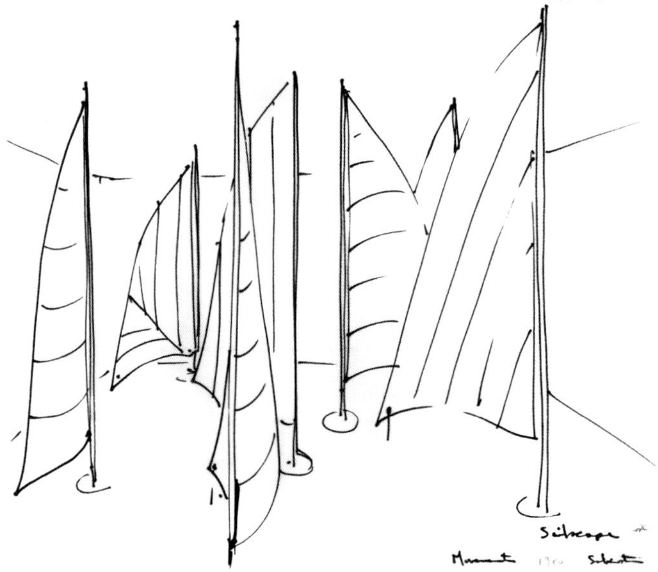

cat. 35 *Studies for Sailing #1, #2*, 1982

cat. 44 *Weather Systems*, 2000

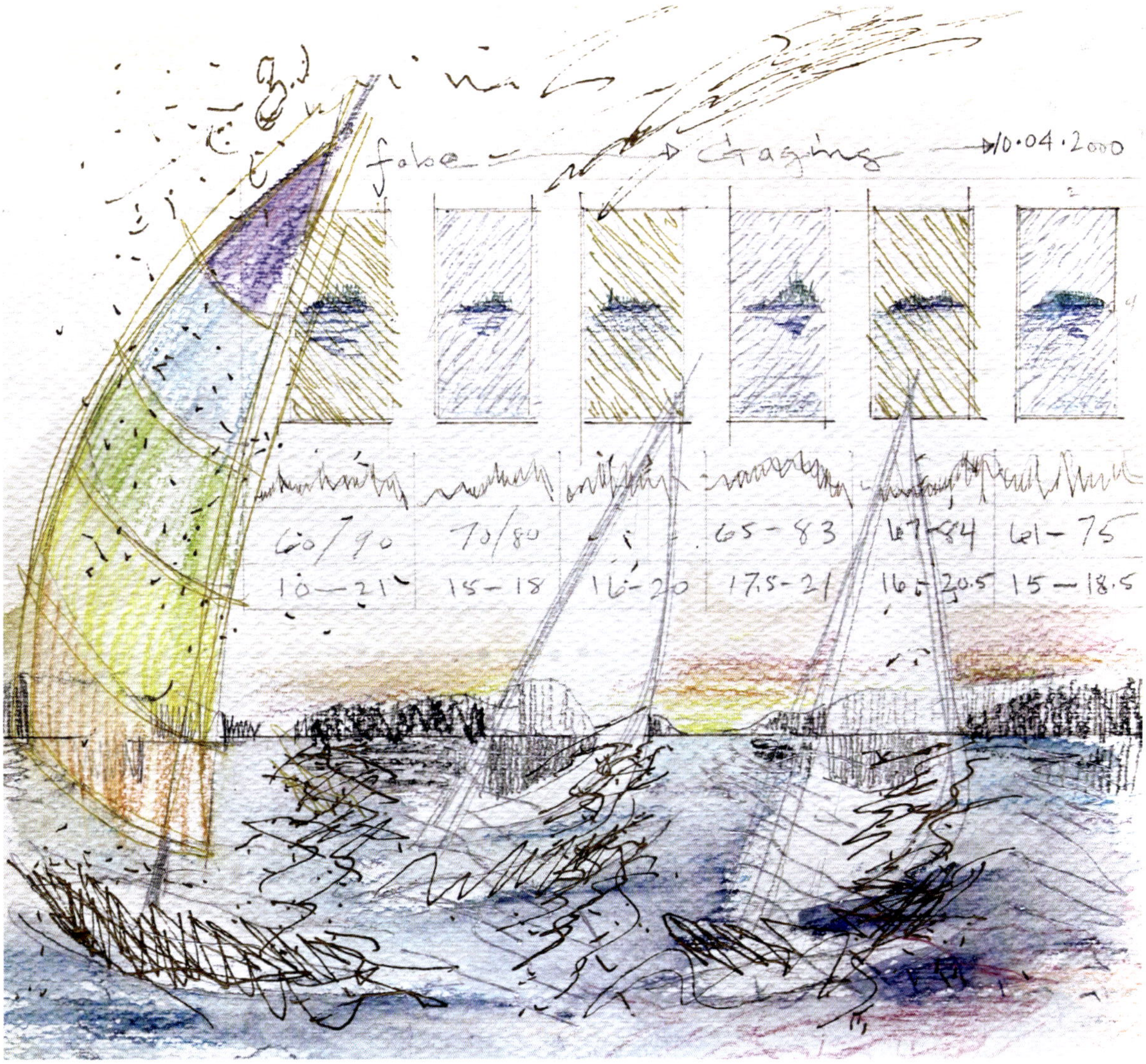

false → staging →10·04·2000
60/90
10–21
70/80
15–18
16–20
65–83
17.5–21
67–84
16.5–20.5
61–75
15–18.5

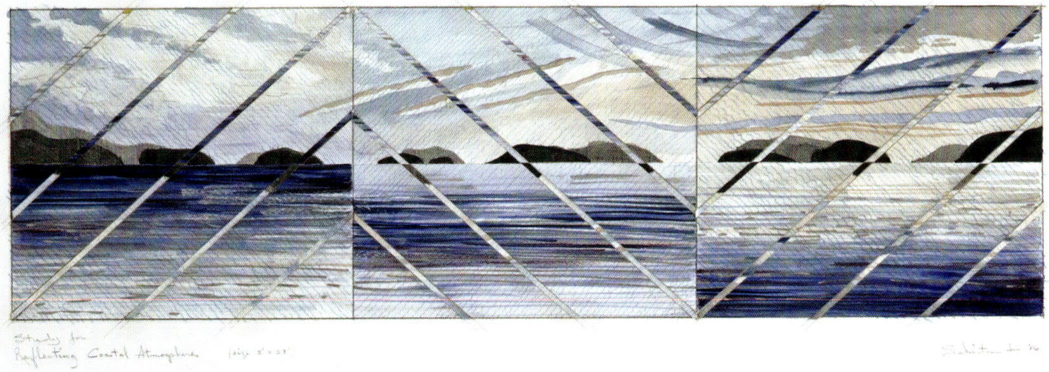

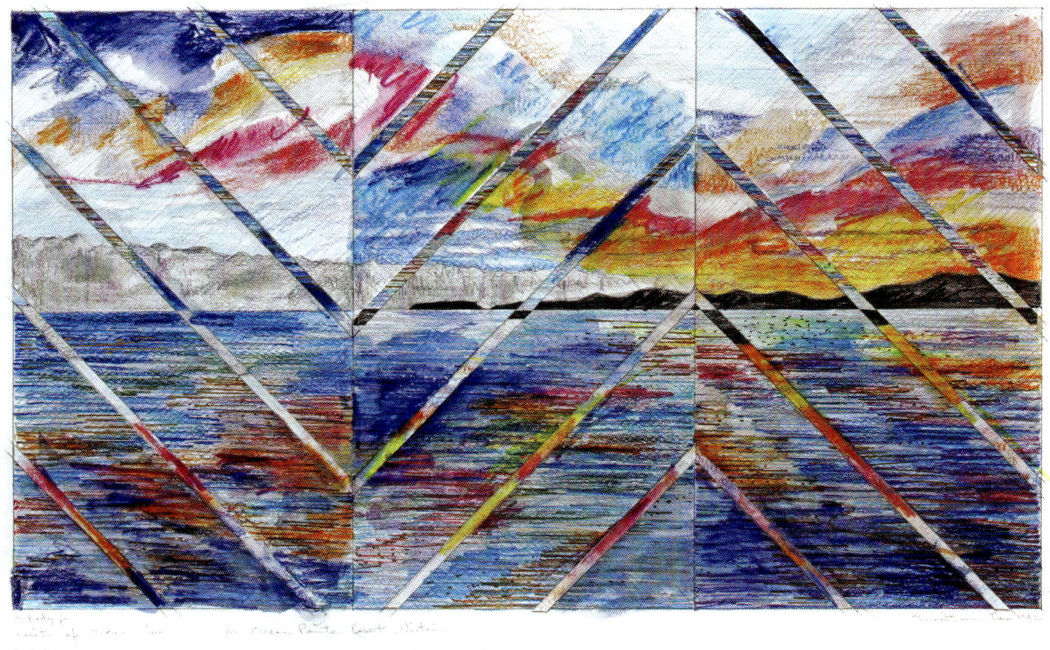

cat. 36 *Study for Reflecting Coastal Atmosphere*, 1986

cat. 43 *Study for Points of Ocean View*, 1992

cat. 42 *Coastal Turbulence #2*, 1985/86

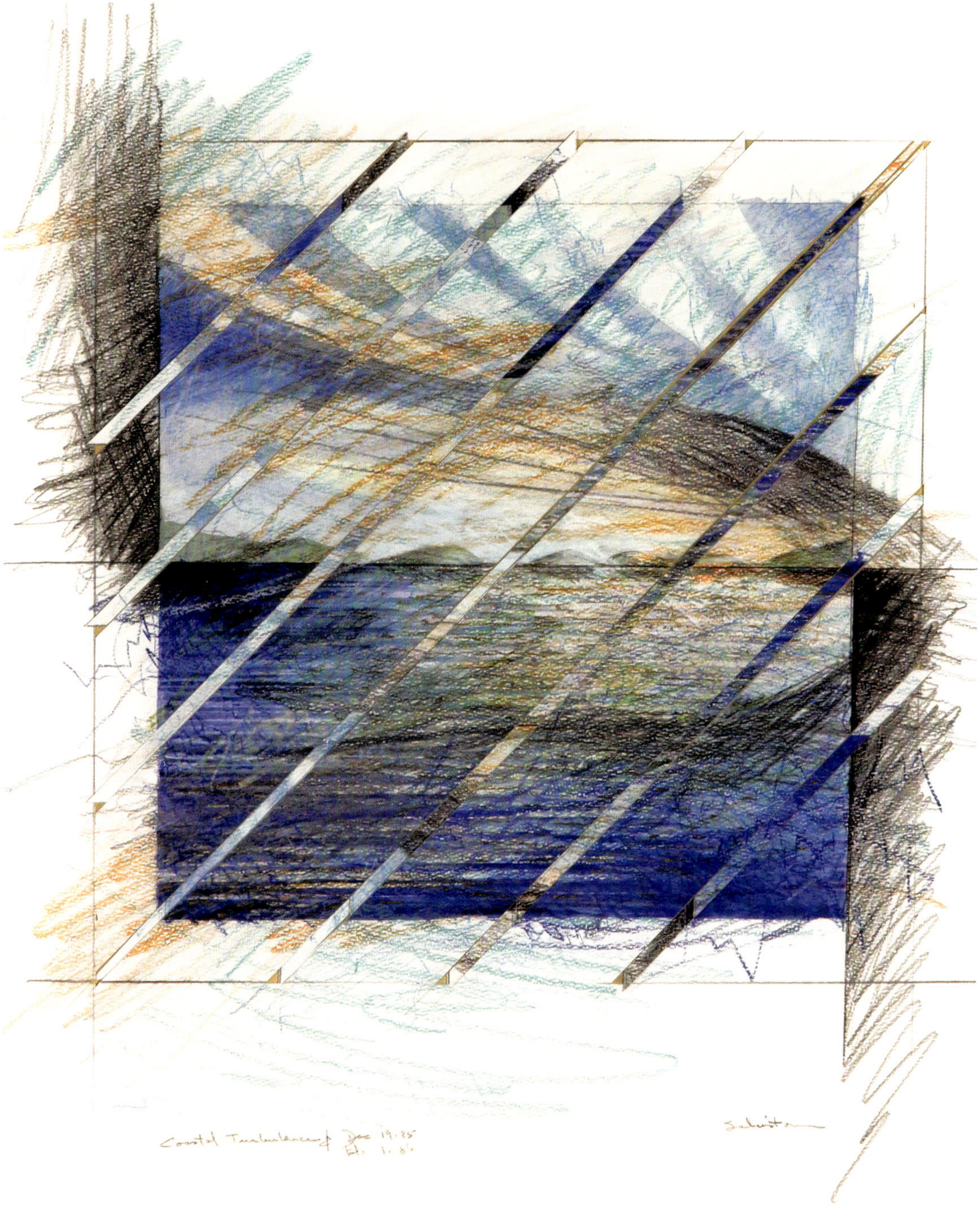

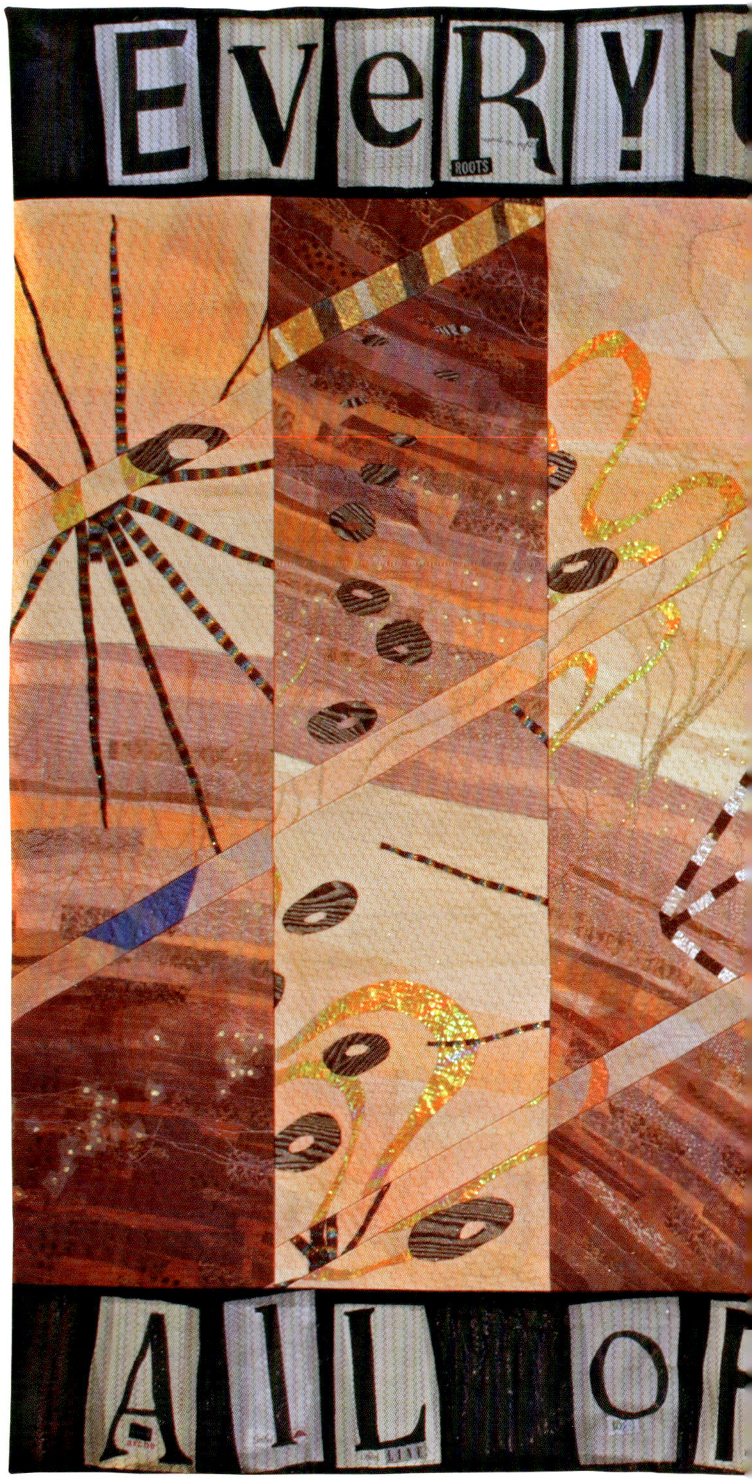

cat. 25 *Everything Below: All of the Above*, 2003

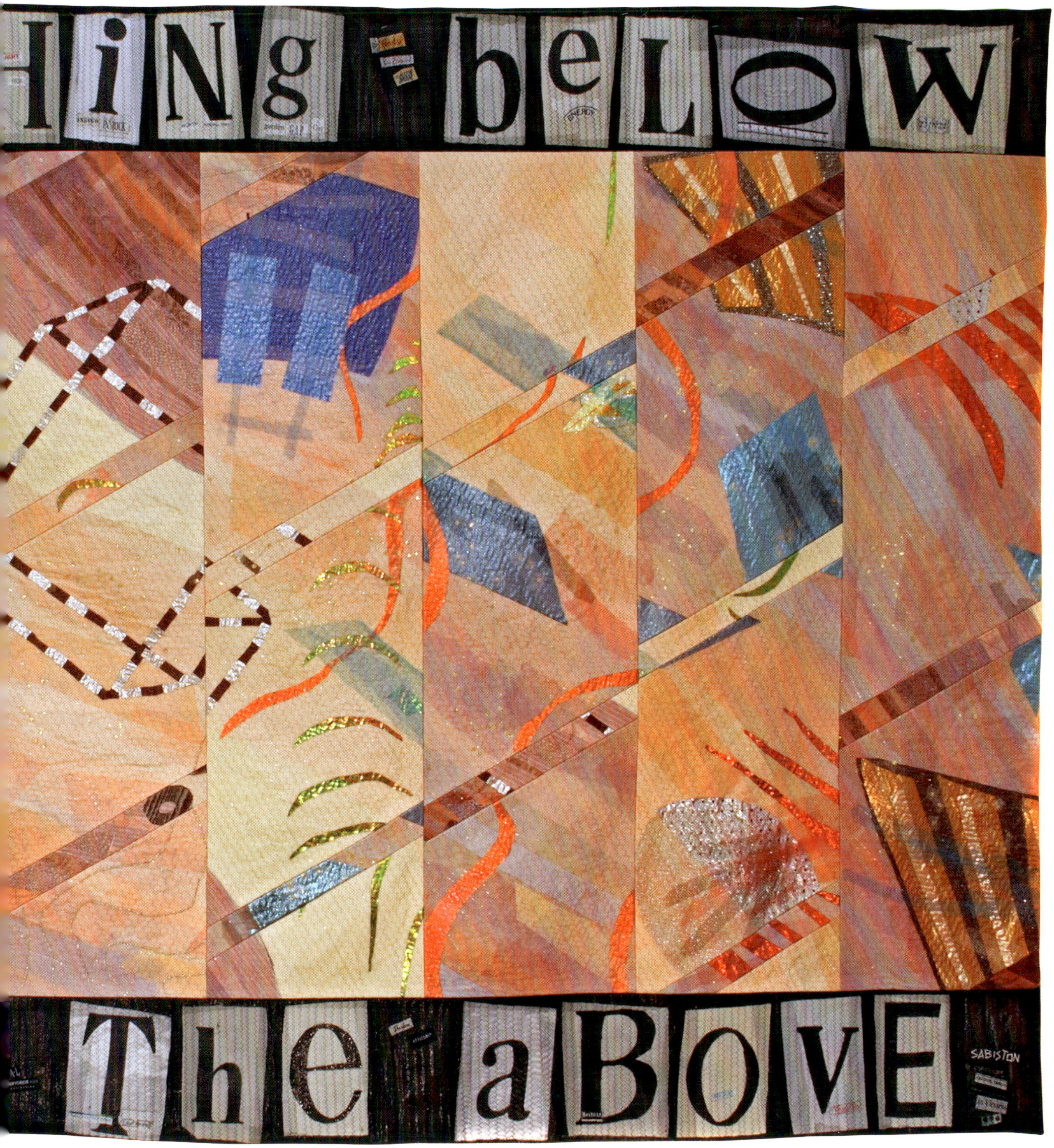
hiNg beLOW
The aBOVE
SABISTON

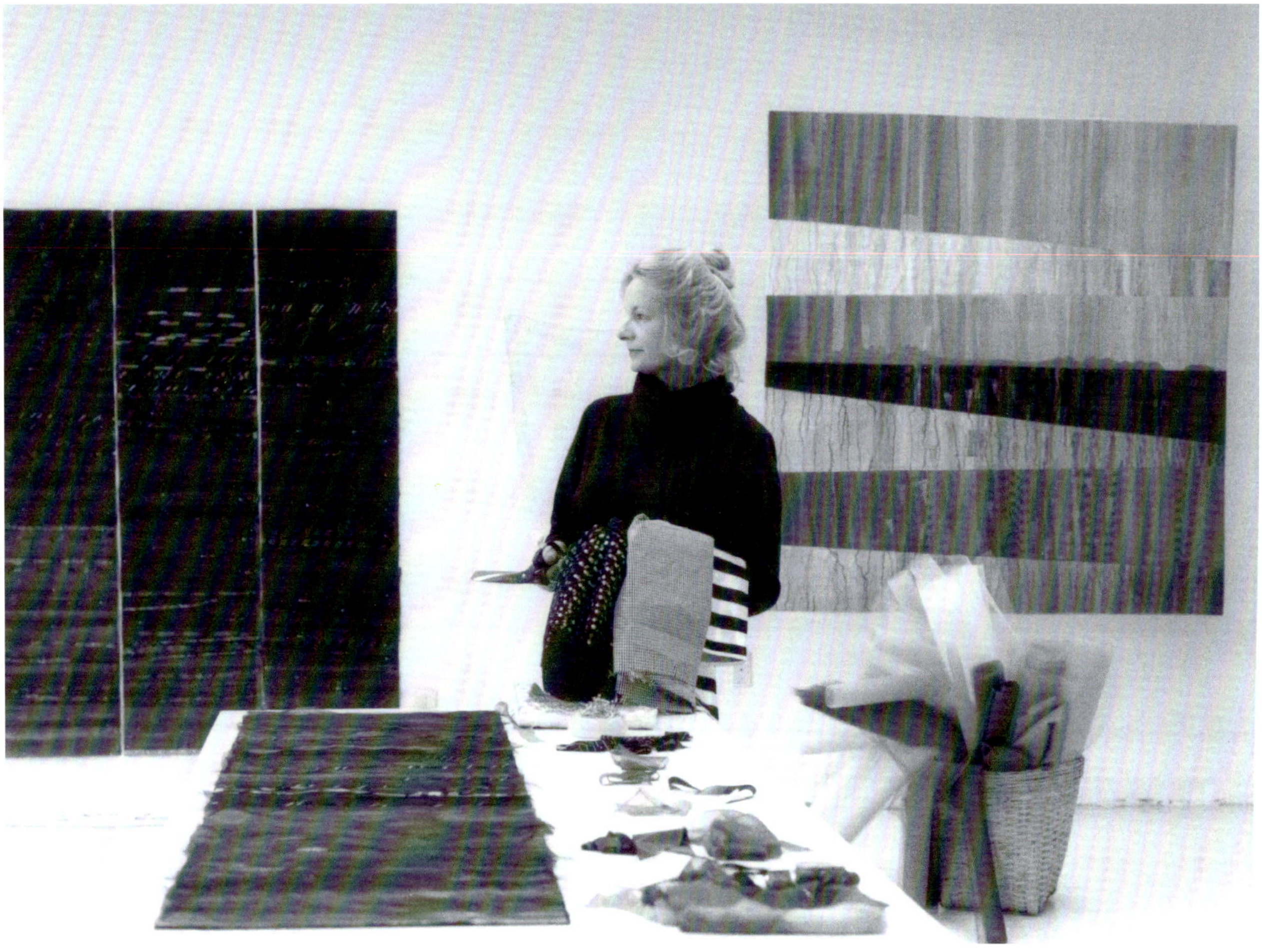

Carole Sabiston in the Studio, 1985

List of Works

Photography by John Taylor unless otherwise noted.

TEXTILE ASSEMBLAGES

1. *Myriad Voices*
1973
hand-stitched
155 x 132 cm
Collection of the Artist

2. *Colour Study: Blue Rain*
1976
hand-stitched
33 x 20.5 cm
Collection of the Artist

3. *Colour Study: Red Garden*
1976
hand-stitched
24 x 19 cm
Collection of the Artist

4. *Japan Journey*
1979
five-panel textile assemblage
305 x 305 cm
Collection of the Artist

5. *Phabulous Phabrics*
1979
upholstery sample book
60.9 x 46.9 x 7.6 cm
Collection of the Artist

6. *Moving Through a Fragmented London Life*
1981
textile assemblage
305 x 305 cm
Collection of the Canada Council Art Bank, Ottawa
Photographer: Brandon Clarida

7. *Sailing: Dotti O'verdose; All That Glitters*
1982
textile assemblage, dress, stockings, and beach rock
305 x 213.3 cm
Collection of the Art Gallery of Greater Victoria, Gift of the artist
Photographer: Stephen Topfer

8. *Sailing: Victorian Secondhand Sail; New-raw-tick Dawn*
1982
textile assemblage and beach rock
305 x 213.3 cm
Collection of the Art Gallery of Greater Victoria, Gift of the artist
Photographer: Stephen Topfer

9. *Living in an Island*
1984
mixed media, net, fabric, coloured pencil, watercolour
101.7 x 76.1 cm
Collection of the Art Gallery of Greater Victoria, Harold and Vera Mortimer-Lamb Purchase Fund
Photographer: Stephen Topfer

10. *Royal Fireworks Suite*
1984
textile assemblage
152.4 x 213.3 cm
Collection of Munro's Bookstore, Victoria
Photographer: Jeff Barber

11. *Self Portrait: The Cocktailer*
1984
mixed media and textile assemblage
62.2 x 50.8 cm
Collection of the Artist

12. *Self Portrait: The Supermarketer*
1984
mixed media and textile assemblage
62.2 x 50.8 cm
Collection of the Artist

13. *Self Portrait: The Suntanner*
1984
mixed media and textile assemblage
62.2 x 50.8 cm
Collection of the Artist

14. *Self Portrait: The Traveller*
1984
mixed media and textile assemblage
62.2 x 50.8 cm
Collection of the Artist

15. *Islands in Colour II*
1986
textile assemblage
152.4 x 152.4 cm
Collection of BC Government House, Victoria

16. *Spatial Possibilities: Dissecting an Examination*
1987 and 1994
textile assemblage
292 cm x 289 cm
Collection of the Artist
Photographer: Jeff Barber

17. *The Flying Rondels At Dawn*
1987
textile assemblage
151.1 cm diameter
Private Collection, Victoria

18. *Spatial Possibilities: Individual Take Off*
1988
textile assemblage
274.3 x 274.3 cm
Collection of Glenlyon Norfolk School, Victoria
Photographer: Jeff Barber

19. *Black's Island / Ice Lake Misted*
1990
textile assemblage
152.4 x 457.2 cm
Private Collection, Victoria

20. *Two Bits of Sky: Day and Night*
1990/91
textile assemblage
216 x 94 cm
Collection of the Canadian Museum of Civilization

21. *Flying into Delos*
1992
textile assemblage
182.8 x 670.6 cm
Private Collection, Toronto

22. *Magicus Carpetus: Squadron—Preserving a Flying Tradition*
1992
textile assemblage & Mason preserve jars
Various dimensions
Private Collections, Victoria

23. *Points of Ocean View*
1992
textile assemblage
182.8 x 548.6 cm
Collection of the Art Gallery of Greater Victoria, Gift of the Ocean Pointe Hotel, Victoria
Photographer: Stephen Topfer

24. *Flying Revolution Quartet*
1993
textile assemblage
91.4 x 91.4 cm
(each quadrant)
Private Collections, Winnipeg and Victoria

25. *Everything Below: All of the Above*
2003
textile assemblage
71 x 110 cm
Collection of the Artist

26. *Flying Rufus*
2009
textile assemblage
120 x 104.7 cm
Collection of the Artist

27. *Flight Patterns*
2009
textile assemblage and dress patterns
60.9 x 91.4 cm
Collection of the Artist, courtesy of Winchester Galleries

28. *Fly the Horizon*
2009
sketch using textile and paper
121.9 x 60.9 cm
Collection of the Artist, courtesy of Winchester Galleries

29. *Opus #1: In the Key of ?*
2009
textile assemblage and keys
45 x 60.3 cm
Collection of the Artist, courtesy of Winchester Galleries

30. *Connecting Threads: Arc of Carol Shields*
2013
textile assemblage
114.3 x 91.4 cm
Collection of the Artist

31. *Planet Earth: After P. K. Page*
2013
mixed media, textile and paper (with the author's permission)
121.9 x 121.9 cm
Collection of the Artist

32. *Pockets for Men's Trousers*
2013
textile assemblage, text and Plexiglas
177.8 x 81.2 cm
Collection of the Artist

DRAWINGS

33. *Studies for Madama Butterfly: Colour Ranges*
1981
watercolour on handmade Japanese paper
52 x 17.1 cm
Collection of the Artist

34. *Studies for Madama Butterfly: Costume for Madama Butterfly*
1981
watercolour on handmade Japanese paper
50.8 x 17.1 cm
Collection of the Artist

35. *Studies for Sailing #1, #2*
1982
ink on paper
29 x 34 cm
Collection of the Artist

36. *Study for Reflecting Coastal Atmosphere*
1986
preparatory study for Canada Trust Bentall IV Building, Vancouver
gouache on paper
68.5 x 89.5 cm
Collection of the Artist

37. *Flying Carpets Study #1*
1990
gouache, silver and gold ink felt pen on paper
57.8 x 68.6 cm
Collection of the Artist

38. *Flying Carpets Study #3*
1990
gouache, silver and gold ink felt pen on paper
57.8 x 68.6 cm
Collection of the Artist

39. *Flying Carpets Study #4*
1990
gouache, silver and gold ink felt pen on paper
57.8 x 68.6 cm
Collection of the Artist

40. *Flying Carpets Study #5*
1990
gouache, silver and gold ink felt pen on paper
57.8 x 68.6 cm
Collection of the Artist

41. *Coastal Turbulence #1* (study for BC Government House work)
1985/86
gouache and graphite on paper
68.5 x 57.78
Collection of the Artist

42. *Coastal Turbulence #2* (study for BC Government House work)
1985/86
gouache and graphite on paper
68.5 x 57.78
Collection of the Artist

43. *Study for Points of Ocean View*
1992
gouache on paper
55.8 x 72.6 cm
Collection of the Artist

44. *Weather Systems*
2000
coloured pencil, black, gold and silver ink felt pen
28 x 30 cm
Collection of the Artist

Chronology

Born in England in 1939. Immigrated to Canada in 1948 with her parents. Studied Fine Art at the University of British Columbia and at the University of Victoria.

SOLO EXHIBITIONS

2009 *Carole Sabiston: New Works*, Winchester Galleries, Victoria, BC

1995 *Carole Sabiston: Transitions*, Winchester Galleries, Victoria, BC

1990 *Carole Sabiston*, Winchester Galleries, Victoria, BC

1990 *Flying*, Art Gallery of Greater Victoria, Victoria, BC

1989 *Sailing*, Memorial University, St. John's, NL

1989 *Sailing*, Anna Leonowens Gallery, Nova Scotia College of Art and Design, Halifax, NS

1985 *Sailing*, Winnipeg Art Gallery, Winnipeg, MB

1984 *Sailing*, Two Rivers Art Gallery, Prince George, BC

1982 *Sailing*, Art Gallery of Greater Victoria, Victoria, BC

1981 Open Space Gallery, Victoria, BC

1979 Open Space Gallery, Victoria, BC

1979 Centre des arts visuels, Montreal, QC

1979 University of Alberta Art Gallery, Edmonton, AB

1975 Bau-Xi Gallery, Victoria, BC

1974 Shaw-Rimmington Gallery, Toronto, ON

1973 *Carole Sabiston: Wall Hangings*, Art Gallery of Greater Victoria, Victoria, BC

1970 Shaw-Rimmington Gallery, Toronto, ON

1968 *Stitcheries by Carole Sabiston*, Art Gallery of Greater Victoria, Victoria, BC

GROUP EXHIBITIONS

1996–1998 *Transformation: Prix Saidye Bronfman Award 1977–1996*, organized by the Canadian Museum of Civilization, travelled to the Musée des beaux-arts, Montreal, QC; Art Gallery of Ontario, Toronto, ON; Winnipeg Art Gallery, Winnipeg, MB; Art Gallery of Greater Victoria, Victoria, BC; Canadian Craft Museum, Vancouver, BC; Art Gallery of Nova Scotia, Halifax, NS; American Craft Museum, New York, NY

1995 Art Gallery of Greater Victoria, Victoria, BC

1993 *7th Montreal Tapestry Biennial*, Montreal, QC

1992–1994 *Celebrating the Stitch: Contemporary Embroidery of North America*, Japan; United Kingdom; Dallas, Chicago, Boston, Seattle, USA

1992 *Wendy Toogood, Jane Kidd, Carole Sabiston: Spatial Illusions: Form and Structure in Fabric*, The Museum for Textiles, Toronto, ON

1988 *5th Montreal Tapestry Biennial*, Montreal, QC

1988 *Restless Legacies*, Winter Olympics, Calgary, AB

1984 Harbourfront Gallery, Toronto, ON

1981 London Regional Art Museum, London, ON

1980 Maltwood Museum, University of Victoria, Victoria, BC

1978 *Made By Hand '78*, Art Gallery of Greater Victoria, Victoria, BC

1977 Ontario Crafts Council, Toronto, ON

1975 Vancouver Art Gallery, Vancouver, BC

1974 Vancouver Art Gallery, Vancouver, BC

1974 Heller Tapestry Gallery, London, UK

1973 Canadian Guild of Crafts, Montreal, QC

1972 Royal Ontario Museum, Toronto, ON

1972 Canadian Guild of Crafts, Toronto, ON

1967 Canadian Guild of Crafts, Toronto, ON

1967 London Regional Art Museum, London, ON

1965 London Regional Art Museum, London, ON

COLLECTIONS

Art Gallery of Greater Victoria, Victoria, BC

Canada Council Art Bank, Ottawa, ON

Canadian Airlines International, Calgary, AB

Canadian Museum of Civilization, Hull, QC

Claridge Collection, Montreal, QC

Confederation Arts Centre, Charlottetown, PEI

Government of British Columbia

University of Victoria, Victoria, BC

Private and corporate collections in Canada, United States of America, United Kingdom and European Union

OPERA & THEATRE PROJECTS

1977–1987 Kaleidoscope Theatre for Children, performed in British Columbia, Alberta, Manitoba, United States of America and Japan, two months (Director, Yukio Sekiya)

1977–1986 *Kaleidophonics* with symphonies in Edmonton, Hamilton, Calgary, Vancouver, Victoria and Winnipeg

1980 Canada Opera Piccola

1974, 1977, 1981, 1988 Pacific Opera Victoria, including *The Magic Flute, Madama Butterfly*

1973, 1974 Company One Theatre

AWARDS

Queen's Diamond Jubilee Medal, 2012

Distinguished Artist, City of Victoria, 2002

Queen's Silver Jubilee Medal, 2002

Distinguished Alumni Award, University of Victoria, 1998

Ambassador of the Arts Award, MISSA, Metchosin, BC, 1997

University of Victoria Honorary Doctorate, 1995

Order of British Columbia, 1992

Canada 125 Medal, 1992

Royal Canadian Academy, Elected Member, 1987

Saidye Bronfman Award, 1987

PUBLIC COMMISSIONS

BC Government House, Victoria, BC, 2007, *Reflections at Government House*

Christ Church Cathedral, Victoria, BC, 2002, *Reredos*, dedicated by Queen Elizabeth II

Royal Jubilee Hospital Hospice, Victoria, BC, 2001, *Safe Harbour*

P.D. James' home, Suffolk, UK, 2000, *Southwold*

Unitarian Church, Victoria, BC, 1999, *Our Beautiful Blue Planet*

Municipal Hall, Police and Fire Headquarters, Saanich, BC, 1997, *Locate*

BC Cancer Clinic, Royal Jubilee Hospital, Victoria, BC, 1996, *Coast Light*

Ocean Pointe Resort, Victoria, BC, 1992, *Points of Ocean View* (now in the Collection of the Art Gallery of Greater Victoria)

Commonwealth Games, Victoria, BC, 1991-1994, *Commonwealth Games Cape of Many Hands* (half in the Collection of the Greater Victoria Public Library, half in the Collection of the Kuala Lumpur National Museum)

Queen's Quay, Harbourfront, Toronto, ON, 1990, *Two Dragons*, 65' each

Cadillac-Fairview, Yonge Corporate Centre, Toronto, ON, 1989, *Shallow Pond* and *Deep Pond*

EXPO '86, Opening Ceremony, Vancouver, BC, 1986, *Sunburst Design*

4 King Street West (Yonge & King), Toronto, ON, 1986, *Spatial Possibilities: Ruby Red Planet; Harvest Gold Planet; Blush Pink Planet* (All Destroyed)

BC Government House, Victoria, BC, 1986, *Islands in Colour I & II*

BC Pacific Forestry Research Centre, Government of Canada, Victoria, BC, 1986, *Three Tree Banners*

Red Cross House, Victoria, BC, 1985, *Curved Island Horizon*

Munro's Books, Victoria, BC, 1984, *Four Seasons Suite*

McPherson Theatre, Victoria, BC, 1984, *Phoenix Theatre Curtain*

University of Victoria Faculty Club, Victoria, BC, 1984, *Transiting Spheres*

Canada Trust Company, Vancouver, BC, 1981, *Howe Sound Suite* (now in the Collection of the University of Victoria)

Westin Bayshore Inn, Vancouver, BC, 1980, *Primeval Forest*

University Centre Auditorium, University of Victoria, Victoria, BC, 1977, *Acoustical Installation*

Ministry of Health, Government of BC, Victoria, BC, 1976, *Transitions*

Sunnybrook Extended Care Hospital, Toronto, ON, 1974, *Untitled*

Christ Church Cathedral, Victoria, BC, 1974, *Advent Altar Frontal*

El Panama Hosteriero, Skyline Hotel, Panama, 1972, *Untitled*

Skyline Hotel, Heathrow Airport, London, UK, 1971, *Untitled* (disappeared)

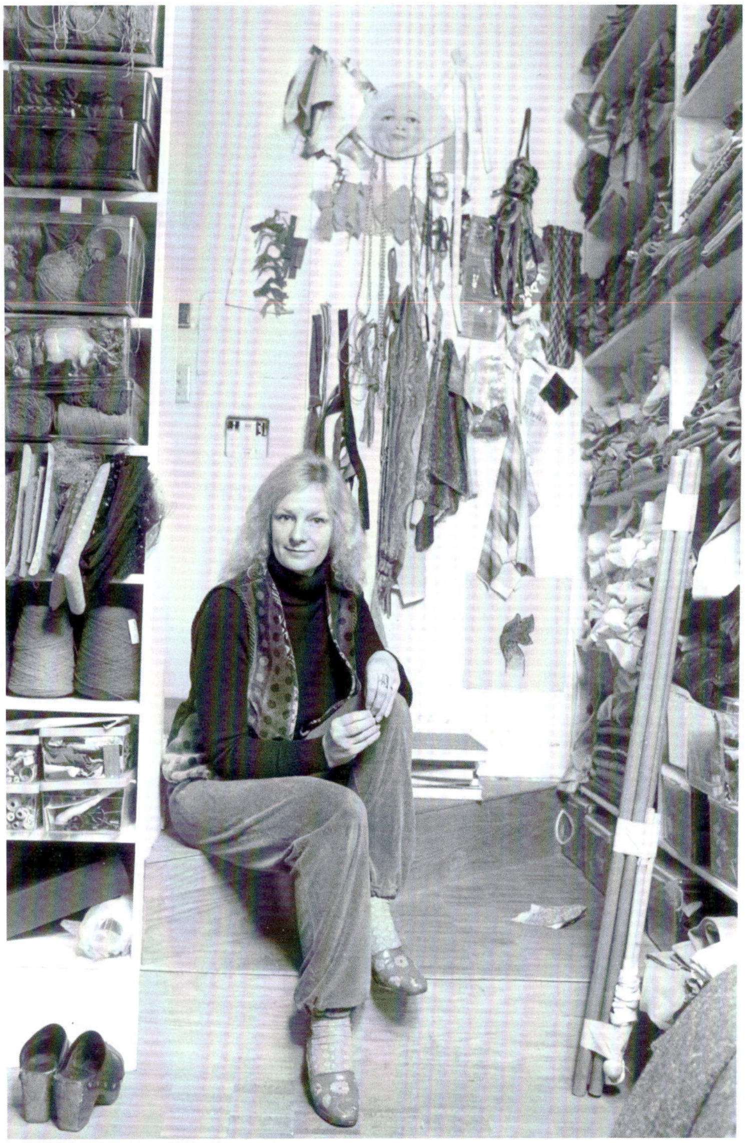

Carole Sabiston in the Studio, 1978

Selected Bibliography

Alfoldy, Sandra. *The Allied Arts: Architecture and Crafts in Postwar Canada*. Montreal and Kingston: McGill-Queen's University Press, 2012.

Amos, Robert. *Artists in Their Studios.* Victoria: TouchWood Editions, 2007.

———. "Carole Sabiston." *Times Colonist* (Victoria), April 7, 1990, pp. C1, C4.

Art Gallery of Greater Victoria. *Art on Video: The Art of Carole Sabiston*. Victoria: Art Gallery of Greater Victoria, with University of Victoria and Knowledge Network (BC), TV Ontario, 1990.

Bellerby, Greg. "Carole Sabiston's Sails: An Expression of the Interaction of Sea and Land." *Fiberarts,* vol. 10, no. 3 (May/June 1983): pp. 17–18.

Bovey, Patricia E. "Carole Sabiston: The Artist's Reflections on 'Flying' and 'Take Off: Point of Departure and Mode of Travel.'" *InSight: A Magazine about Contemporary Art* (Art Gallery of Greater Victoria), Summer 1990.

———. *Carole Sabiston: Flying*. Victoria: Art Gallery of Greater Victoria, 1990.

———. *A Passion for Art: Art and Dynamics of the Limners*. Victoria: Sono Nis Press, 1996.

Bristol, Pam. "Carole Sabiston 1987 Bronfman Winner." *CraftNews,* vol. 12, no. 5 (July 1987): p. 1.

Cassels, Lynda. "The Multi-Textured World of Carole Sabiston." *B.C. Woman*, vol. 8, no. 9 (September 1993): pp. 24–26.

Dean, Ankaret. "Imaginative 'Planet' Hangings Are Constructed on Huge Scale." *Toronto Star,* July 26, 1986, p. L11.

Elder, Alan C., Stephen Inglis and Sandra Flood. *Transformation: Prix Saidye Bronfman Award 1977–1996*. Gatineau, QC: Canadian Museum of Civilization, 1998.

Fox, Mary. "Carole Sabiston, Exploring the Art of Theatre." *British Columbia's Western Living*, vol. 8, no. 2 (February 1978): pp. 22–24 and cover.

———. "The Victoria Galleries." *British Columbia's Western Living*, vol. 5, no. 7 (September 1975): pp. 18–20.

Gould, Jan. *Women of British Columbia*. Surrey, BC: Hancock House Publishers, 1975.

Hartog, Diana. "Layer upon Layer." *Monday Magazine*, January 10–16, 1985, pp. 8–10.

Johnson, Audrey. "A Fertile Creativity in Full Flower." *Victoria Times*, August 27, 1977, p. 21.

———. "Inventive Minds Combine for Pacific Opera's Flute." *Times Colonist* (Victoria), January 30, 1987, p. C6.

———. "Picture a Whole Gallery Filled with Sails." *Times Colonist* (Victoria), September 11, 1982, p. C6.

Knott, Edith. "The Art of Fabricating Motion." *Islander Magazine (Times Colonist)*, June 7, 1992, p. M1.

Kritzwiser, Kay. "Making 'Galactic Fantasies' from Fabric." *The Globe and Mail*, September 23, 1986, p. D8.

Litwin, Grania. "Artist Recycles Fabric of Society." *Times Colonist* (Victoria), September 16, 1984, p. C1.

———. "Shimmering Reflections Covers 'Tacky' Mirrors." *Times Colonist* (Victoria), April 14, 2007, p. C7.

McIlroy, Randal. "Shape Gives an Additional Twist to Sabiston's Work." *Winnipeg Free Press*, February 2, 1985, p. 18.

Piper, David. "Canada: Dimensions 1969." *Crafts Horizons*, vol. 29, no. 5 (September/October 1969): pp. 28–31, 70.

Richards, Jean. "Cloth Is Artist's Tool." *Edmonton Journal*, February 22, 1979, p. B13.

Rogers, Linda. *The Broad Canvas: Portraits of Women by Women.* Victoria: Sono Nis Press, 1999.

Sabiston, Carole. "Conjuring up a New Life." In Carol Shields and Marjorie Anderson (eds.), *Dropped Threads 2: More of What We Aren't Told* (pp. 293–302). Toronto: Vintage Canada, 2003.

Smith, Barbara Lee. *Celebrating the Stitch: Contemporary Embroidery of North America.* Newtown, CT: Taunton Press, 1991.

Tovell, Vincent, producer. *Ties That Bind: Fibres.* Hand & eye series, part 6. Toronto, ON: Canadian Broadcasting Corp., 1984.

"Un art qui prend le large." *L'Illustré* (Lausanne, Switzerland), no. 11 (March 13, 1985): pp. 110-111.

The Wade Williams Partnership. "University Centre, University of Victoria, British Columbia." *Canadian Architect*, vol. 23, no. 9 (September 1978): pp. 26–32.

Wigod, Rebecca. "Not a Small Body of Work, By Any Stretch." *Times Colonist* (Victoria), May 27, 1986, p. C1.

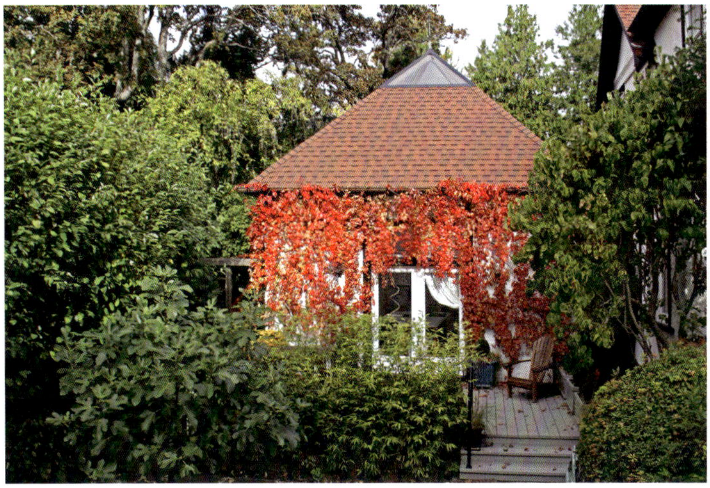

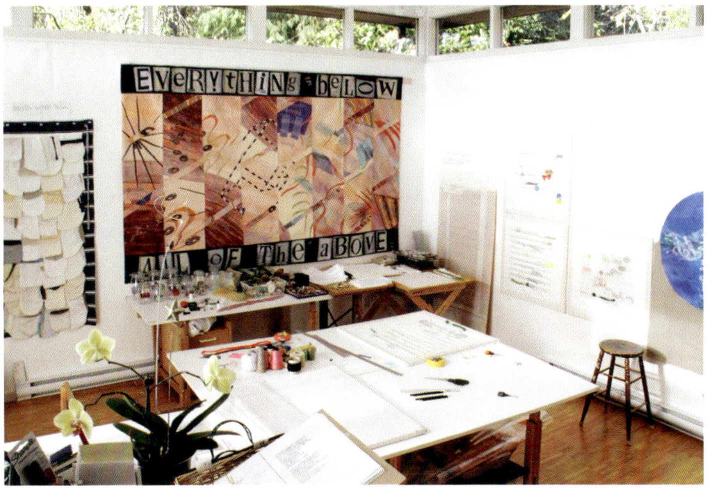

Carole Sabiston's Studio, 2013

Credits

Exhibition curator: Patricia E. Bovey

Contributing writer: Michelle Jacques

Art Gallery of Greater Victoria coordinator: Michelle Jacques

Publication project manager: Michelle Jacques

Editor: Audrey McClellan

Publication designer: Frank Reimer

Photographer: John Taylor, except where noted

Printed in Canada by Friesens Corp.

Gallery Associates
ART GALLERY OF GREATER VICTORIA

British Columbia Arts Council
An agency of the Province of British Columbia

Canada Council for the Arts
Conseil des arts du Canada

CRD
Making a difference...together

1040 Moss Street
Victoria, British Columbia
Canada V8V 4P1
aggv.ca
250-384-4171

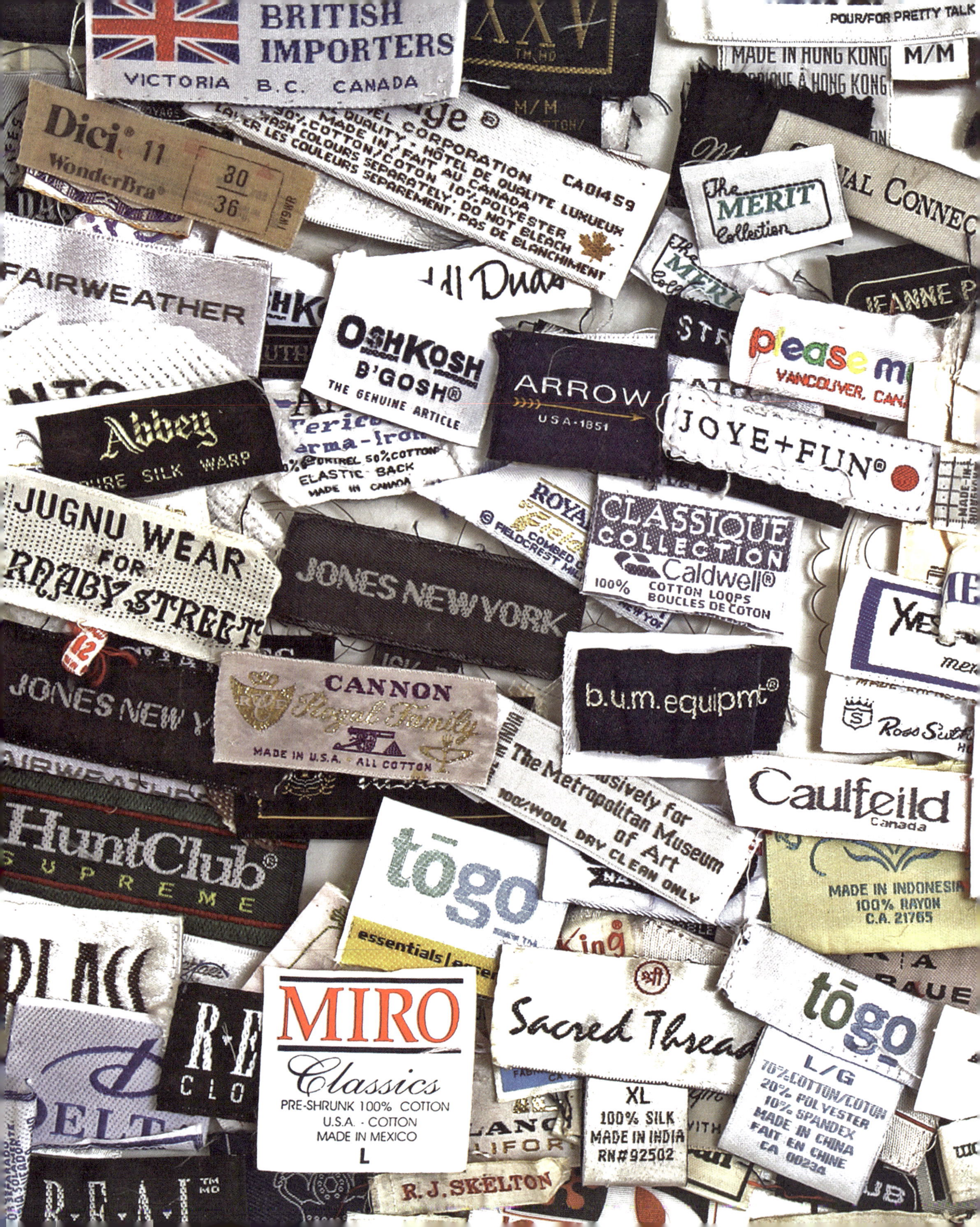
BRITISH IMPORTERS
VICTORIA B.C. CANADA
POUR/FOR PRETTY TALK
MADE IN HONG KONG
M/M
Dici 11
WonderBra
30
36
CA01459
The MERIT Collection
FAIRWEATHER
OSHKOSH B'GOSH THE GENUINE ARTICLE
ARROW USA-1851
please m
VANCOUVER, CAN
Abbey
JOYE+FUN
ELASTIC BACK
MADE IN CANADA
JUGNU WEAR FOR RRABY STREET
JONES NEW YORK
CLASSIQUE COLLECTION
Caldwell
100% COTTON LOOPS BOUCLES DE COTON
CANNON
Royal Family
MADE IN U.S.A. ALL COTTON
b.u.m.equipmt
The Metropolitan Museum of Art
100% WOOL DRY CLEAN ONLY
Caulfeild Canada
HuntClub SUPREME
tōgo
MADE IN INDONESIA 100% RAYON C.A. 21765
MIRO Classics
PRE-SHRUNK 100% COTTON
U.S.A. - COTTON
MADE IN MEXICO
L
Sacred Thread
XL
100% SILK
MADE IN INDIA
RN#92502
tōgo
L/G
20% POLYESTER
10% SPANDEX
MADE IN CHINA
FAIT EN CHINE
R.J.SKELTON